THE PROCESS OF
LANDSCAPE DESIGN

THE PROCESS OF
LANDSCAPE DESIGN

Seamus W. Filor

B.T. Batsford Ltd · London

Acknowledgements

Typeset by Goodfellow & Egan Ltd., Cambridge and printed in Great Britain by Courier International Ltd., East Kilbride, Scotland

Published by B. T. Batsford Ltd
4 Fitzhardinge Street, London W1H 0AH

A CIP catalogue record for this book is available from the British Library

ISBN 0 7134 5751 1

The contents of this book are the result of interviews and discussions with many people, too numerous to mention individually. The assistance of two institutions was invaluable. The University of Edinburgh has given me constant support during my research, and the Canberra College of Advanced Education provided me with a base during my Australian studies. The Carnegie Trust for the Universities of Scotland generously funded part of the American research costs.

Of the many individuals, I must highlight the Lynch family, Denis Blom, Judith Webster and Tony McCormick in Sydney; John Gray, Adrian Pilton and Cath Wellman in Canberra; Ron Lovinger in Eugene, Oregon, and Basem Shihabi, Zahir Hassan and Mohammed Salama in Ar–riyadh. Most importantly, Jean Gorman in Edinburgh and Olga Turyn in Canberra, who produced the typescript, and John McGovern who printed the majority of the photographs.

Contents

List of illustrations

1

Introduction

The design process

There is a solid body of opinion that the creation of a landscape design follows a definite process: entailing a rational working method; embodying a theory; embracing a range of technologies; and that it is imbued with a set of cultural and ethical values – personal and social. It is also recognized that the element of time is paramount in this process, as the major elements of landscape design are ruled by dynamic changing forces. The land, its mantle of soil, and the vegetation layer upon the soil, respond to natural laws which we ignore or interfere with at our peril. Society, the ultimate client the profession serves, is ever-shifting in its perceived values and aspirations. Goals and purposes can radically shift, new technologies and social patterns develop, overturning both the how and the what in the process of design. More than any other form of artefact design, landscape proposals must take account of these unpredictable changes, and be robust and flexible enough to adapt to and accept future uses and demands. Kevin Lynch has said that we can predict and design for the effects of perceived change, but we cannot reasonably prescribe solutions for the changes which follow on from their initial impact.[1]

This concept of change, of the influence of time on the gradual maturing of landscape design, has been acknowledged by many other authors and practitioners. Laurie suggests that many designs may not be effective for between twenty and thirty years;[2] Colvin points out the need to be looking forward to the long-term outcome of design.[3] Equally, the sites most designers work upon contain elements of some previous design, some structure or pattern conceived, implemented and adapted by previous societies, designers and technologies. Hal Moggridge has dubbed this 'retrospective collaboration across time', with known and unknown designers.[4] There can be few project sites which have not been influenced by some previous user.

There are as many models of the landscape design process as there are landscape designers. However, there are three common components of any project – the site, the purpose to which the site is to be put, and the designer. Each of these will have a bearing on the preferred design solution, varying in degree from one project to another. Arnold Weddle has said that no landscape has a value until it has a purpose,[5] and Kevin Lynch that one site may have different values to different people or professions.[6] Weddle was specifically referring to the visual evaluation of landscape at the regional planning level; for more general purposes he means that the value of landscape or scenery can only be rationalized against a planned change in use, or a concrete development proposal. Then the values of society can be used to make a balanced choice, based on an assessment of loss or gain to the parties affected. To follow the Lynch argument, a site would evoke different responses from a farmer, an ecologist and a property developer, and be exploited and altered in different ways by each person.

The role of the designer in this process is crucial. He or she must arbitrate between the often conflicting demands and needs of interest groups, respect the inherent values of the land, and satisfy his or her own design standards. This is why landscape designers have always worked to a set of design principles, explicitly stated or not, to ensure that their proposals are sensible, rational and artistic solutions to particular problems. The Red Books of Humphrey Repton are precursors of today's project reports, development plan documents and Plans of Management. Similarly, Olmsted wrote widely about the principles – social and artistic – that guided his designs.

Too often the design process is illustrated or imagined as a series of discrete parts, following each other in a set sequence – standard survey, analysis, concept and final design. This drastically simplifies what is in fact an interactive process, where information arising at one particular stage must be tested against facts, goals and issues thrown up at other stages. The pattern is cyclical rather than sequential, like a wheel which is moved clockwise or anti-clockwise as the need arises: 'backwards' to validate a concept against previously established site information, or 'forwards' to monitor a previous, completed project to investigate whether this has achieved its aims in use, and can thus serve as a design precedent.[7] These systematic steps backwards and forwards through the sequential model are a vital ingredient in the process. Without the ability to assess the design problem simultaneously against a range of constraints, that terminal designer virus 'analysis paralysis' can set in, and block

further movement. Each stage in the process is important, but the weight given to each will depend on the character of a particular scheme, and will vary throughout the design period. It is only when the problem to be solved has been identified that pertinent information can be sensibly analysed. Even then the problem is not static, new constraints and opportunities becoming apparent as a particular line is explored. The original problem must then be reformulated, and additional information gathered and evaluated.[8] The difficulty, however, is often one of first breaking into the cycle of the process, of establishing the constraints or parameters within the Problem Space, clearly identifying those aims or issues which are really vital to an understanding, and hence finding a solution to the defined problems. This is usually achieved by a designer's initial conceptualization of a design solution, which can be used as an 'ideal' model against which to test the constraints and opportunities imposed by the site and the requirements of the brief and the users.[9]

Rational, systematic and rigorous testing of any design concept is essential. It is important to see this initial concept as a first step, something which will change, often out of all recognition, as it is evaluated against scientific and qualitative criteria. As Steadman says, 'fundamental questions of design can be illuminated not by any attempt to make the process of designing "scientific", but rather by subjecting the products of design to scientific study.'[10]

This view of the preconceived image was anathema to the design methods movement prevalent in the 1960s where Form had to

follow Function. However, it is now gaining ground in the world of architecture and urban design. Alexander feels that every project must first be experienced and then expressed as a vision seen in the inner eye, so strongly that it can be communicated to others and felt by others as a vision. It must, however, be evaluated against pre-established site and user criteria. Only when it is judged to meet their requirements can the vision finally be accepted and developed as the design solution.[11] Hillier and Leaman believe that the designer's preconceptions 'are exactly what makes design possible at all, and indeed what makes possible the identification of a design in the first place.'[12]

Donald Schon, in his empirical study of the working of design studios in schools of architecture, describes this act as the designer imposing 'his preferences onto the situation in the form of choices whose consequences and implications he must subsequently work out – all within an emerging field of constraints'.[13] Schon defines this step as problem-setting: an often undescribable set of procedures and rules by which designers set limits within the finite Problem Space, establishing design goals or issues which will begin to structure the problem, and lead to solutions. These problem-setting limits or constraints arise through a process Schon describes as 'reflections-in-action', that stage in the design process known to all practitioners when ideas and concepts are tested against site constraints and the requirements of the brief, on the drawing board or, increasingly, on the CAD screen.[14]

It would be misleading to regard all design solutions as springing fully formed from some vision – heavenly or otherwise. Often they arise as a combination of the ideal and the practical. Thus it may be constraints such as land form or soil condition which generate the concept. By wrestling with the technical problems inherent in these – the means – a spatial, aesthetic solution may suggest itself – the ends. In this process the individual designer does not distinguish one step or process from the other. Rather they are bound intimately one to the other.

In such instances problem-setting, ends and means are reciprocally determined. And often, in the unstable world of practice, where methods and theories developed in one context are unsuitable to another, practitioners function as researchers, inventing the techniques and models appropriate to the situation at hand.[15]

Having established the role of the preconceived image in the design process, it is important to return to the cyclical model and discuss the element of design against an extending timescale, introduced earlier. This has long been recognized by landscape designers as the main factor which sets their profession apart from other applied designers. Indeed, for many landscape architects it is through an unravelling of the dynamic natural and human processes which have shaped, and will continue to shape, the site, that they define and solve the design problems. For them, the restoration of damaged land, polluted water or an unhealthy built environment provides the spark, the driving motivation for their design concept and solution. To Patrick Geddes a 'diagnostic survey' of existing buildings and open spaces was the most vital element in his

policy of 'conservative surgery' in rehabilitating overcongested cities.[16] Both McHarg[17] and Hough[18] prescribe a similar survey and recording of the natural processes operating within a city or region. Hough sees the values of urban ecology integrating with social and economic objectives to create a rational basis for design.

The conventions and rules of aesthetics have validity only when placed in context with underlying bio-physical determinants. Design principles, responsive to urban ecology and applied to the opportunities the city provides through its inherent resources, form the basis of an alternative design language . . . whose inspiration derives from a vernacular that makes the most of available resources; one that re-establishes the concept of multi-functional, productive and working landscapes.[19]

For these designers, the element of time – past, present and future – is a component vital to purposeful and beneficial change, with ecology and man as its indispensable base. 'Thus design and maintenance, based on the concept of process, become [no longer] separate and distinct activities, but an integrated and continuing management function, guiding the development of the man-made landscape over time'.[20]

These policies set up their own dynamic set of problems – political, social and of continuing management. Handley has defined the role of a landscape manager as one of maintaining designed landscapes in a position of dynamic equilibrium.[21] Certainly for Hough's design principles to be effectively translated into practice, the landscape manager, whether from the local authority, a

contractor, the community or a voluntary organization, must play a continuing role, beginning at the design stage. Indeed, the method of management would seem largely to dictate the evolving, changing design form. It should therefore be an important element in the design process and the cyclical testing and evaluation of design ideas. The solution to the design problem, the scheme which is agreed with clients, documented and constructed, is thus the result of a continuous interplay between site issues and user issues, a process which continues once the project is constructed and in use.

During the design process, the landscape architect will rigorously research the site constraints and user demands to establish how their spatial, technical and managerial characteristics and standards will shape and influence the evolving design ideas. Some of this information will be provided by other professionals or authorities, but it is important that the landscape designer ensures that this is provided in a form relevant to the particular problem under investigation. Is the data required at the macro or micro level? What are the implications of specific toxic minerals in a soil sample for the uses planned on a site? What is the estimated run-off from roofs and roads in a new neighbourhood and how can this be dealt with to avoid overloading the present natural drainage system? Are there still local craftsmen to construct traditional walls or paving? How well organized is the local nursery industry to provide the range of plants specified? Such questions must be posed and answered by the designer in setting and then evaluating the ever-shifting design problems.

Lynch has conceptualized this in a diagram of shifting objectives. An objective is set, the process of collating and analysing data relative to this begins. However, as data is evaluated it becomes apparent that the initial objective is not wholly desirable, a new one is set, and the process shifts towards meeting this.[22] Jellicoe's terms of reference to his ecology consultant at Sutton Place were 'to study the present ecology of the area between the walled gardens and the fringe farmland, and present scientific proposals as a basis of landscape art'.[23] In this case the designer's sketch design pre-dated the ecological survey, and set constraints within which the survey took place. In turn, the ecological findings modified the forms of both major water features: the lake and the cascades. It is equally important to investigate the implications of the design brief, how facilities can be sensibly accommodated on the site, how users perceive the site and the proposed new uses, and what their real and perceived needs mean in terms of spatial design, artefact provision and retention of symbolic existing features. Research here will involve user surveys, evaluation of similar completed projects, and an initial investigation of the potential impacts of such development on both site and local community.

The need to involve the real users, the people whose daily lives will be most intimately affected by any new development, has been recognized since community opposition, focused mainly against urban redevelopments and motorways, organized itself into forceful lobby groups. Various methods have evolved in an attempt to recognize community aspirations and to

consider these in the design proposals. Landscape architects now make use of sociologists in structuring questionnaires, analysing the results and setting up dialogue with community representatives. They have also developed their own techniques, for observation and mapping of how people use and perceive space and facilities. From his observations of how people use selected plazas in New York, Whyte has suggested design standards for such areas, covering their size, orientation, amount and form of seating and other artefacts which people seem to value.[24] Lynch and Downs have each attempted to involve local people, by asking them to draw a map of their locality and identify elements of particular value or significance to them. Through this, Lynch suggests, a designer can obtain a community image of a particular place to set against his own professional assessment. Through studying commonality and divergence between these images, proposals for the area pertinent to the needs of the locals can evolve.[25]

Over the last twenty years, Lawrence Halprin has developed a process which he calls 'scoring'. This is analogous to the combination of musical notation, stage directions, set and costume design, and group creativity, which the choreography of a modern ballet must embrace. Halprin initially developed his system to choreograph the anticipated sequential movement of people through open spaces he was engaged in designing. From initial personal evaluations for projects such as Nicollet Avenue, experimental interactive creative workshops – 'Experiments in Environment' – involving

students of landscape architecture, architecture and dance, followed later by design-awareness workshops for federal bureaucrats, Halprin and his colleagues developed a system of workshops which they try to use as a preliminary to all their major design projects. At these workshops, community and bureaucratic groups are involved in hands-on exercises to 'score' events, places, actions and activities in their local environment, which can be respected and incorporated into the design process.[26]

To draw this discussion of the Design Process together the next section looks at three separate landscape design projects, to show how a particular, personal preconception has generated the design solution. The common elements to all are water and size. They are otherwise widely separated geographically and in time. The projects are the Water Gardens at Hemel Hempstead, near London (1959), the Levi Strauss Plaza in San Francisco (1978), and the water features at Bicentennial Park in Sydney (1988).

The first of these, the Water Gardens, were designed by Jellicoe as a linear public park, on a narrow strip of land along a small river. This separated the town centre from surface car parks. The initial concept was to widen the river to create a formal canal. Excavated material was mounded on the west bank, to screen the cars and create sloping flower gardens and a narrow footpath. Elegant bridges would connect the car parks to the town centre, across the cascaded canal.

It was then that the serpent, inspired by Klee's two paintings in rich combination ('Highways and

1.1 (Left) **A simple footbridge connects the flower gardens and car parking across the 'Monster's Back' to the town centre. Water Gardens, Hemel Hempstead.**

1.2 (Next page) **The 'Serpent's Tail' presses against the grass hill at the end of the Water Gardens, Hemel Hempstead.**

1.3 (Page 13) **Some 25 years after the construction of the Water Gardens the islands and reeds suggest the ageing skin patterns on the head of the 'Monster'.**

By-ways', 1929, and 'The Vessels of Aphrodite', 1921), was conceived as a complete and balanced form. Thereafter every detail conformed to this idea; the monster head with its single fountain eye and mouth; the flower gardens like a 'howdah' strapped to its back (by the bridges); the underbelly curving almost imperceptibly; the lively tail pressing against a hill – all so abstract as to remain unrecognisable and unseen to the roving eye.[27] (Figs 1.1 and 1.2.)

From Jellicoe's description, this subconscious idea has driven the design concept, transcending the initial technical and circulation constraints to create a work of art derived from an interpretation of Klee's paintings. Returning twenty-five years later to reappraise the project, Jellicoe was satisfied that the concept had generally survived the passage of time. Additional islands and sculpture are likened to 'skin reticulations' and flies on the face of the monster, acceptable signs of an ageing in the friendly beast (Fig.1.3). Extra planting along the underbelly, however, is diminishing the desired contrast between the ornamental flower gardens and the more simple eastern bank.

There are few works so liable to suffer change as parks and gardens. By burying an idea into the water gardens it is hoped that this idea will be its own protection. The form subconsciously aspires to animal perfection and any threat of amputation or deformation would undoubtedly be resisted by the layman, without knowing the reason why.[28]

1.4 **Even without water this fountain and meandering course still evoke the character of a mountain stream. Levi's Plaza, San Francisco.**

Halprin's design for Levi Strauss Plaza is conceived more as an interpretation of a stream, erupting from a mountain waterfall which then meanders between grassy knolls and pathways. The design embraces two threads which characterize much of Halprin's work – the abstraction of the natural ecological form of Californian streams into an artificial urban artefact, and the response to the needs and movement patterns of the users in the layout of the park. At the same time it creates its own special character, a green space insulated from the noise and bustle of the adjacent city streets (Fig. 1.4).

These two designs of Jellicoe and Halprin demonstrate personal concerns which appear constantly in their work: the subconscious influence of fine art for Jellicoe, and in Halprin the moulding of the spatial design to match the movement of people. The third example draws on another theme to spark the design process – historical analogy.

Bicentennial Park in Sydney, Australia will be discussed more fully in chapter 2, in relation to the Parramatta River study. This section relates only to the canalized water feature within the southern, parkland section. For this parkland the designers have used as their model the nineteenth-century urban parks of Europe and America, and the local example of this style, Centennial Park, built in 1888.

As in the plans of Paxton, Kemp, Alphand

1.5 The canal and 'treillage' borrow elements of the design principles current in nineteenth-century park designs in Australia. Bicentennial Park, Sydney.

and Olmsted, a strong formal, axial promenade is contrasted with freer forms of land, planting, paths and water. The designers, however, reject the ethics of these design models, describing their concept more as a celebration and a total acceptance of classical urban design principles, such as order, geometry, focal points and axes. As a consequence the main water feature reflects the major pedestrian link from West Concord station to the State Sports Centre.

The axis (is) planted with multiple avenues of plane trees, and lined with seats. It is started and terminated with vertical water elements linked together with a channel of water 200 metres long . . . At the point of intersection of the two major axes and at the highest point of the park lies a major focal point, the treillage – . . . from which springs the water source for the central canal and the focal point of the Bicentennial Park concept, 200 water jets commemorating each year since settlement, and from which one can overview the

park . . . A manipulation of architecture, trees, water and paving.[29] (Fig. 1.5).

Elements from a previous period or style have thus been reused to bring order and unity to a site perceived by the designers as having no past of its own worth building upon.

What we have now is a new landscape on the old rubbish dump which builds on some of the European traditions that you have in Centennial Park.[30]

This brief comparison of the design concepts underlying three different water features demonstrates that although the initial artistic concept may arise for a variety of reasons – sub-conscious or self-conscious – this is only the beginning of the design process. The image must be tested against the critical and fundamental constraints of site and brief. The personal, subjective vision must prove its worth against technical and cultural criteria before it can be accepted as a sensible solution to the problem set.

Another area of research for a model to generate an initial design step is the study of previous examples from the same problem area – similar 'types' of problem, with similar requirements or standards to meet, may be expected to produce similar solutions. To examine the logic of this there follows a brief study of some precedents, or types, similar to the five main case studies used in the book, to test whether the identification of commonality between similar functions is useful. Rowe has stated that a type, which is itself one thing, stands for or represents more than one thing. 'Our trees and their trees are all "tree".'[31] For example, sports fields can be expected to have broadly similar characters, and Environmental Impact Assessments follow a common set of procedures. Thus a designer would expect to study previously completed projects of a similar type, to analyse or monitor how the 'typical' problems have been resolved.

The aim of this book is to examine how established landscape projects, on a variety of scales, with different uses and in a range of cultures, have evolved over time. Five main case studies are used as vehicles. They each represent a particular type of project, which occurs in many other places. Each demonstrates special influences on the design solution – aspects of the natural environment, a distinctive society and culture, and different levels of economic commitment. The interaction between these various elements during both design and project implementation, and subsequent to completion, is described and evaluated against the initial design goals and management principles. The projects are: landscape planning; urban regeneration; new town development; university campus design; and winter sports development.

LANDSCAPE PLANNING

To take the first of these: it is probably erroneous to label landscape planning as a 'type', covering as it does such a wide variety, scale and complexity of projects – Environmental Impact Statements for area-wide and point subjects; land-use planning and resource management for aspects such as watershed management and re-afforestation; recreation planning and management; and urban expansion policies. The role of the landscape designer will also vary from project to project, depending on the particular issues involved. Sometimes he or she will play the lead role of Project Manager, formulating a strategy, co-ordinating and evaluating the work of other specialists and authorities, and producing the final document. More usually, however, the landscape designer will act as a consultant for particular aspects within the study, under the leadership of another professional.

In 1977 the British Institute of Landscape Architects debated a change of title and branches of membership, to recognize the breadth of expertise required to successfully design, establish, and ensure the longevity of, landscape projects. At one stage the job of Landscape Planner was considered a separate skill alongside Design, Management and Science. However, the membership felt that the skills of Landscape Designer and Landscape Planner were too similar to be separated, varying only in degrees of scale and complexity. This is true up to a point: the processes of scoping and screening in an EIS study, the techniques of matrices and overlaying for organizing and analysing information, and the skills of visual survey and appraisal, are all similar to stages in project design, as also is the vital aspect of monitoring. Evaluation of EIS projects subsequent to their completion, to test if they are actually meeting their stated standards, is regrettably too often lacking. This is relevant not only to individual project performances:

such testing of actual performance standards provides valuable feedback for subsequent EIS Reports.[32] Increasingly, however, the term 'Management' has become more applicable than 'Planning', particularly in countryside topics. The policies set out in many plans are no longer finite – if they ever were – but establish a baseline record of the environmental condition of the study area and set out various options for change, each with a balance of loss or gain. Management, rather than planning, is increasingly being emphasized, to focus and co-ordinate the actions of landowners, resource developers and statutory authorities. Documents must now be more comprehensible to non-professionals, they must be understood and agreed to by the local community and entrepreneurs, and be open-ended enough to accept later adjustments or shifts in policy.

The Parramatta River Study was such a document. Some fifteen years after publication, it is still referred to and used by local and state politicians and officials, and by professionals undertaking projects within the study area. It has been described as the first true example of landscape planning in Australia.[33] (Figs. 1.6 and 1.7.)

1.6   **Native planting on an old industrial site. Kelly's Bush Park, Parramatta River, Sydney.**

1.7 **A new jetty at Banjo Patterson Park, Parramatta River, Sydney. The poet's restored house is the centrepiece of the new park.**

1.8 *(Opposite, left)* **Orange Way Park, Boston, USA. This linear park lies on top of a new Metro line. It creates a continuous green finger, creating opportunities for community gardens, sports fields, sitting areas and pedestrian links.**

1.9 *(Opposite right)* **Traffic management and environmental improvements by Glasgow Planning Department have revitalized this local landmark. Bridgeton Cross, Glasgow.**

URBAN REGENERATION

Rebuilding and regenerating run-down and decayed urban areas, the second case type, has a long and well-documented history. Currently there is a strong reaction to the post-Second World War policies of slum clearance and comprehensive redevelopment. There has been a return to formulas similar to the 'conservative surgery' expounded by Geddes over eighty years ago.[34] Eckbo suggested how the US 'Superblock' could be re-adapted, and made more suitable for family living, a concept developed by the Barcelona Ajuntement in their plans for the 1992 Olympic Village.[35] These policies combine minimal demolition and new build with restructuring of circulation routes and rehabilitation of existing structures.

Open space has been recognized as an important element of urban regeneration, in upgrading the physical appearance of an area to encourage subsequent development, providing a setting for new or renovated buildings. Also, permanent open space is seen as a catalyst to attract new businesses, industries and housing into decayed areas, with temporary treatment of potential development sites to eliminate eyesores (Fig. 1.8).

Garden Festivals have been used as economic catalysts in Germany, Holland and Britain. In Britain such festivals last for six months, act as a focus to attract Government and corporate finance, and restore a run-down area to park use, or attractive development land. The multiplier effect of a festival also boosts tourism to areas previously unattractive to visitors, and encourages future commercial and industrial developers.[36]

Heritage is also being developed as a tourist and educational resource in these old, previously disregarded areas. The growing interest in urban studies and in industrial archaeology has spawned a plethora of visitor centres and theme trails, interpreting the past for today's citizens.

The Glasgow Eastern Area Renewal (GEAR) project is a useful illustration of an attempt to revitalize one such run-down urban area. Located in the largest urban area in Scotland, the project set out to break the cycle of decline in employment, population, and health and housing standards.

During the initial ten years of its life, landscape architects were involved in a range of projects, some of which are described in chapter 3 (Fig. 1.9).

NEW TOWN DEVELOPMENT

UK new town policies, established in the 1950s, have been criticized for accelerating the decline of older industrial urban centres, and creating the problems which GEAR set out to solve. Indeed, the two new centres of Cumbernauld and East Kilbride have been accused of drawing off many of the younger, more employable sections of Glasgow's population, their light and service industries replacing the older employers such as steel and shipbuilding. They were, however, an important catalyst in creating a genuine team approach to urban design.

After the initial planning techniques of survey, analysis and the like, the actual design process of creating the master plan began with the arrangement of three elements: the land, the building groups and the means of communication between them. The arts of landscape architecture, architecture and road architecture coalesced to become a new element, a new scene, the townscape.[37]

Each of the British new towns developed a personal character, a result (according to Gibberd) of their topography, the individuality of their development corporations, and the imagination of their designers. It is interesting that Gibberd has put landscape architecture as first of the arts involved in new town design. Landscape designers were involved from the beginning in the preparation of Master Plans for all the British new towns, and continued to control the implementation of projects as the towns developed. Their influence in establishing criteria for the form of the Master Plan is apparent, especially in terms of existing landscape features – Gibberd particularly mentions the role of topography. A comparison of the two Scottish towns of Cumbernauld and Livingston shows contrasting responses: Cumbernauld crowning a hilltop, with fingers of afforestation tying it back to the lower valley forms; Livingston huddled within the valley, the centre overlooking the linear river park, the existing agricultural shelter belts reinforced by hill-top woodlands. Cumbernauld was envisaged as a tight, urban settlement, gaining protection from the elements by the architectural form, Livingston as being much looser, fitting into the established rolling landform and agricultural pattern.

Other factors have sparked the designs of Milton Keynes and Warrington. Milton Keynes has been called the City of Trees, as a result of its policy of large-scale tree planting to complement and integrate the ubiquitous 1km road grid. This grid planting, often supplemented by earth mounding, increases privacy for adjacent dwellings, and reduces headlight glare and the visual intrusion of car movement. The grid roads are perceived as 'rural' roads, where 'control of landscape offers the major opportunity to provide visual continuity, aid navigation, and reinforce the enjoyment of scale, form and the movement in the city as a whole . . . a landscape policy where design is generated by major topographical features and sector scale planning'. The planting, by subsequent management, will be 'edited' to emphasize particular views which help the driver in orientation, navigation and perception of the total city.[38]

At Birchwood in Warrington, the ground conditions played a large part in the design and management concept. The site had been a munitions factory, covered with concrete foundations, bunkers and railway lines, with any surviving soil severely compacted. Landscape reclamation techniques largely dictated the design policy; the rubble and clinker from rail beds formed shelter mounds, while sub-soil and waste material were the planting medium. Separate areas were assessed as to their capacity to support vegetation, and compatible species and planting techniques were developed for each. The result may be seen as an example of accelerated habitat creation. The new landform was designed to accommodate the required housing areas and community facilities, while interesting existing habitats were set aside and managed as wildlife areas. This policy has largely worked, because the land was reclaimed several years ahead of the housing development. This allowed the designers to experiment with various planting and establishment techniques, and meant that the vegetation was reasonably mature and robust by the time the houses were occupied.[39]

Similar techniques of planting, imposed by

harsh climate, limited water budget and poor growing medium, have dictated the design policy for the new town built as the Diplomatic Quarter at Ar-riyadh in Saudi Arabia. Here the concept followed has been one of concentrating scarce irrigation water in the central core of the development, and using only drought-resistant, largely native, plants in the remainder of the town. This policy has created a successful blending of the town into the adjacent sparsely vegetated plateau. The project is also an interesting example of close co-ordination between client and designer to achieve a design solution compatible with environmental, social and cultural needs (Fig.1.10).

1.10 A desert landscape has been created around the Diplomatic Club, in the Diplomatic Quarter, Ar-riyadh. Native plants do not need irrigation once established.

UNIVERSITY CAMPUS DESIGN

University campus planning, another case type, has been used by both Laurie and Lynch as a model to illustrate the design process.[40] The involvement of landscape architects in campus design has a long history: Capability Brown remodelled the Backs at Cambridge to create a setting which unified a disparate collection of college buildings, and Repton was similarly involved at Oxford, with Magdalen College. Geddes and Walter Burley Griffin were interested both in designing an educational plan and locating a fitting site for universities at Jerusalem and Canberra, whilst Olmsted greatly influenced the character of the rural, Land Act Universities established in the US in the 1860s.[41]

The original European universities, which grew out of monastic institutions, reflected the form of their parents – a collegiate system based on cellular courtyards or quadrangles. The tradition continued in the colonies, in America and elsewhere, and remained the dominant form into this century. Olmsted's concept for the new Land Act universities proposed an alternative form of individually-sited buildings, responsive to the topography and with expansion potential, and students living in domestic-scale accommodation.[42] This responsiveness to site has often influenced the development and academic plans of universities.

On the other hand, the site chosen may inspire the educators to modify their academic objectives so that a positive contribution can be made to programme development. One example of this is the beautifully wooded site at the University of California, Santa Cruz, which encouraged the development of small residential college clusters rather than the larger-scale, departmental groupings found at other campuses in the state system.[43]

In a campus design process, the users to be considered are the students and the faculty – academic, research, and service staff. As economic pressures continue to force universities to develop alternative incomes and to increase their levels of fee-paying students, the character of the campus plays an increasingly important role.

It was the buildings, the trees, the walk-ways, the well-kept lawns, that overwhelmingly won out. The appearance of the campus is, by far, the most influential characteristic during campus visits, and we gained the distinct impression that when it comes to recruiting students, the director of buildings and grounds may be more important than the academic dean.[44]

This clearly establishes the need for a continuing commitment to the maintenance and management of the campus and to a clearly defined set of goals. The University of Stanford, whose total campus extends to some 3200 ha, only a small percentage of which is built on, has developed a complex system of integrated policies and plans directed towards continuously improving the quality of the campus. They have established an environmental ethic which sets out to balance academic needs against landscape resources. Some nine separate campus-wide plans cover: land-use; circulation and parking; street furniture; lighting; vegetation management; outdoor scientific use, to utilize parts of the campus for teaching and research; landscape character assessment; landscape guidelines for future developments; and a study of heritage features. The breadth of this coverage demonstrates Stanford's commitment to ensuring that their landscape resources continue to play a major role in one of the most dynamic universities in the US.[45] The case study of Stirling University describes how the academic and development plans were influenced by the site, and how that realized plan has responded to changes, in both academic and management areas (Fig. 1.11).

1.11 **Stirling University campus, seen from the south.**

DEVELOPMENT OF COUNTRYSIDE
FOR RECREATION

The scenic quality of landscape and its potential as a resource to be exploited has a long tradition. The early National Parks in Canada and Australia were developed by the railway companies, as sites for hotels linked to countryside recreation. Banff in Alberta and the Mount Kosciusko and Royal National Parks in New South Wales were all examples of this. Indeed, much National Park and countryside legislation is bedevilled by the inbuilt contradiction of trying to preserve natural resources and at the same time ensure access and enjoyment for visitors. This conflict between user and resource often results in the destruction, or at least a deterioration, in the quality of the resource. There is clearly a role for landscape design at all levels of countryside planning – establishing policies for development and management; locating suitable, least-damaging sites; designing actual projects; monitoring the short and long-term impact of these on the environment; and reappraising policies in the light of these findings.

These problems will relate, in varying degrees, to all sites which attract a large number of visitors and their vehicles: the coast and lakes for water sports; hills to climb and ski on; heritage sites such as archaeological monuments, battlefields or historic homes; attractive and accessible countryside to drive through and picnic in. Problems of habitat destruction, soil erosion, water pollution and incompatible structures are common and must be foreseen and catered for by policy, design or management. At the same time the economic benefits which such developments can bring to often declining areas must be recognized.

The case study chosen is a ski resort in Colorado, US, which also has facilities for summer sports – hill walking, fishing, horse riding and latterly golf. Winter sports developments provide an extreme example of the opportunities and problems inherent in any countryside recreation development. The environment is invariably very fragile, with delicate vegetation, thin, easily erodible soil, extreme climate, heavy rainfall and high winds to accelerate erosion, and a short growing season which limits the ability of the vegetation to repair itself. These factors are further exacerbated by the impact associated with downhill skiing itself. The sport is generally channelled onto particular runs, which are daily groomed by piste machines. These compact the snow, and hence the underlying vegetation and soil. The landform and vegetation are altered to accommodate the runs. Slopes are regraded, rocks blasted, trees removed. Ditches are dug for drains and to carry the services for snow-making machinery. Pylons must be constructed for the tows, chairs and lifts to carry skiers to the runs. Restaurants, ski hire facilities, hotels and car parks must all be built to service the thousands of daily visitors. Power and water must be provided and waste disposed of.

To justify such heavy investment in buildings, uplift and servicing, the resorts must operate all the year round. One effect of this is often that the chair-lifts are made to carry many more visitors to the upper slopes, where their trampling feet increase the damage to the vegetation, resulting in often incongruous but necessary solutions. For example, at Threadbo, in Mount Kosciusko National Park, a raised steel mesh walkway has been erected across the plateau. Similarly at Cairngorm, in the Scottish Highlands, the route from the top of the chair-lift to the summit has been paved. These urban intrusions into areas of high scenic quality are consequences of continuous visitor use. Before the chair-lift, summer use was limited to genuine hill walkers, and the impact consequently much less. Now the mechanical lifts make it possible for people of all ages and physical fitness to share the experience of these high places. At the same time, however, they are contributing to a deterioration in the quality of the resource, and this is the dichotomy which countryside planners must resolve. Telluride, through a close collaboration between developer, resource manager and landscape architect, consciously attempted to minimize these conflicts, and to ensure that the resource continues to be enjoyed by the widest possible range of users.

2

Landscape planning
The Parramatta River Study

In the early days of colonial settlement in Australia, the Parramatta River was the main link between the administrative and commercial base at Sydney Cove, and the initial agricultural hinterland developed around Parramatta. Gradually commerce and industry developed around suitable landing sites on the river to handle both imports and exports. With the spread of urban and suburban Metropolitan Sydney and the move from water-based to land-based transport, the river corridor became less important. Industry, no longer dependent on the river, turned its back on it. The growing suburbs faced their road access, and largely ignored the water frontage. Access to the foreshore was generally limited, and the recreational potential of the river apparent only to a few bodies and individuals.

In 1974 the New South Wales branch of the National Trust of Australia convened a meeting of local riverside councils and statutory authorities to discuss co-ordinated action for the rehabilitation of the river. This meeting established the Parramatta River Conservation Co-ordination Committee (PRCCC). The committee obtained funding from the Federal Department of Urban and Regional Development for a comprehensive study of the Parramatta River. The study report, *Parameters for the River*, was published in July 1975.[1]

The purpose of this chapter is to see how the findings and recommendations of the report have affected the riverside environment over the last 13 years; it will briefly describe the aims, methodology and findings of the report, then discuss its effects and influence on the subsequent environmental changes to the river. Finally, it will look in more detail at some new authorities and legislation that affect the river environment, and at recent projects – recreational, industrial and residential – to evaluate their responses to the Report's recommendations (Fig. 2.1).

THE STUDY

The consultants – Lynch, Spence and Pearson – concentrated their original research on an inventory and appraisal of visual qualities and recreational opportunities. Other important factors, such as water quality, habitat structure and socio-economic impacts, relied on existing data. Consultant botanists and ecologists reviewed the current literature, and concentrated their field work on obvious gaps in this. From the beginning the Report was seen as a means to an end, not a meticulously presented prescription for the rehabilitation of the river. It was a synoptic gathering together of data from the geographic catchment of the river. The natural systems of the river landscape rather than municipal administrative boundaries were used as the data-gathering base. The need to involve the community, as well as their elected and appointed representatives, in a continuing process of decision making was stressed. To

Legend:
———— Major roads
– – – Railway
1. Harbour Bridge
2. Darling Harbour
3. Mort Bay, Balmain
4. Iron Cove
5. Birkenhead Point
6. Quarantine Station
7. Wellcome Site
8. Walker Hospital
9. Wangal Reserve
10. Homebush Bay
11. Bicentennial Park
12. Banjo Patterson Park
13. Silverwater

2.1 **A map of the Parramatta River.**

this end, a sociologist described and evaluated three possible methods by which the community could be involved. The Report was structured into two parts: 'Description and Analysis'; and 'Ways and Means'.

The aim was to inform decision makers and lobbyists of the factors that have shaped, and will continue to shape, the visual, biological, social and cultural state of the Parramatta River. Armed with this knowledge of the interrelated causes and effects of environmental change, all the parties involved are in a position to formulate and evaluate a range of possible actions before deciding on a particular course. Under 'Description' fall four further broad sections: the river as a consequence of natural processes; the compromised natural systems, or how the remnant natural systems relate to a new riverscape; urban phenomena, a discussion of the history, people and land-use in the river valley as a background to rehabilitation; and the river experience, an analysis of the character, form and perceived qualities of the water course and its new hinterland.

Throughout Part One ('Description and Analysis'), the Report isolates particular 'factors' and 'issues' that derive from this general discussion of the river valley's characteristics. Factors establish the values – natural, urban or perceived – against which change within the river corridor may be measured. Issues are specific aspects that affect these factors and consequently require attention. For example, one 'factor' influencing the compromising of natural systems is economic and recreational viability of a biologically healthy river system. Two 'complementary issues' are the unrecognized

potential of the river for elementary biological teaching and wildlife observation; and the reduction of maintenance that will result from selecting indigenous species for replanting programmes. The factor indicates a value decision, the issues indicate latent opportunities for achieving or enhancing this value: the first issue would involve school teachers and voluntary wildlife groups in developing a potential educational and recreational resource on their doorstep, the second indicates possible financial savings as an inducement to landowners to plant species native to the area. All these issues are ranked in order of priority for attention at the end of Part One, together with an indication of the party most concerned with their implementation. A key aspect in naming priorities was the need to involve the community. At the same time it was seen as essential to isolate those issues which, if not promptly dealt with, would lower the value of the river to an extent where community choice or alternatives were reduced. Another consideration was to identify issues with little or no community interest or involvement, and direct these to the responsible authority for early action. A scale matrix was used in the ranking process. This was based on four critical determinants, each further subdivided to reflect increasing levels of complexity.

Three groupings of issues were formed, 'Recommendations', 'Alternatives' and 'Considerations', ranging from most to least critical. The first 'grouped issues' – those needing a 'recommendation strategy' – include both broad aspects of biological vulnerability and small design improvements to existing sites. For instance, the advantage

of conserving mangrove in inter-tidal areas that other species cannot tolerate is noted; whilst the impediment to waterside use created by playing-field fencing represents a different highlighted issue.

At the second level of grouped issues are those that require alternative strategies. These are seen as both less critical and less readily soluble than the first group. There is also a recognition of the need to involve the community in developing these strategies. For example, 'Alternative Five' couples the issue of river views screened from bridges by signs and barriers with the dilution of existing views from roads by roadside clutter and inappropriate planting.

The final grouped issues were those for 'further consideration'. This brought together issues which related to long-term trends, such as changing patterns in recreational activities, or to policy decisions made at Federal Government level. These grouped issues fell well beyond the scope of the report and were simply presented to the relevant authorities as 'considerations'.

At the conclusion to Part One of the Report, the issues are stated as problems or opportunities. Specific sites or enabling authorities are not identified. Part Two, 'Ways and Means', sets out to rationalize defined options for river improvement requiring action from the community and relevant authorities. It develops the grouped issues by defining specific actions, sites or organizations that can positively influence each of the concluding recommendations, alternatives and considerations. A matrix correlates each of these in turn to 13 separate 'rehabilitation parameters', which relate to the data described in Part One, covering aspects such as access, land-use, planting, historical and natural conservation, education and administration (see Fig.2.2). To supplement this matrix, a series of paired plans cover the area of the river corridor.

The first set identifies sites with conservation value and suggests aids towards their conservation – for instance habitats such as mangroves and salt marsh – and geological features. Conservation aids refer to specific areas that would benefit from management as wildlife habitats, and include possible interpretation sites and the involvement of schools in river rehabilitation.

The second set of plans, comprises a diagram of 'planning choices'. This indicates locations of potential water use, park development, land access, riverside scenic road improvements and complex areas needing detailed planning action by the statutory authorities.

The final section of Part Two is almost an enabling handbook, which suggests methods of systematically involving the community and recovering sites and property for river-related functions. It also gives technical guidelines on park development, shore improvement and riverside planting.

These technical guidelines, together with the conservation values and planning choices, are to be read alongside the tabulated recommendations, alternatives and considerations. Together they document the actions required to achieve the overall rehabilitation of the Parramatta River. The 10 recommendations indicate a need for immediate action; the 17 alternatives suggest potential medium-term actions; and the 5

considerations identify broad areas of concern requiring long-term National level action.

The Parramatta River study did not set out to produce a classic master plan with future functions absolutely defined and spatially structured. Rather, it aimed to present the river as an integrated system with a particular set of values that must be respected if rehabilitation is to succeed. Rehabilitation and conservation are merely tools to promote an increase in the usefulness and attraction of the water and its foreshore for a growing number of local people. Recreation, in its broadest sense, is seen as the main force in returning the river system back to community use. Buildings for industrial and residential use will continue to dominate a majority of the views obtained of the corridor, but over time they will be better integrated with the riverscape fitting into the views from land and water, and providing access along and to the water at previously inaccessible points.

Potential areas and opportunities were identified and general design guidance regarding planting, artefacts and water-edge details was given. However, no actual site proposals were developed beyond these levels. This was to ensure that no arbitrary design decisions were taken before the main values and issues outlined in the Report were fully considered both by the communities affected and by the relevant authorities and landowners.

In 1975 the Parramatta River was identified as a neglected and polluted resource but one offering great recreational, educational and cultural potential for the local communities. The next part of this chapter describes what

has happened to the river over the 15 years since the Report was published and assesses the influence of the values and issues identified in it.

The value of the Parameters Report has been recognized by various individuals and authorities in the years since publication. It has been referred to by several subsequent studies and has been instrumental in focusing the work of at least one council towards the rehabilitation of the Parramatta River. Some 15 years after publication, the biological health of the river has improved remarkably, foreshore access and boat-launching facilities have increased, ferry services have expanded, new public parks have opened and industry is attempting to be a better riverside neighbour (Fig.2.3).

2.2 **Correlation index. This matrix stratifies the 13 rehabilitation parameters into three classes: recommendations, alternatives and considerations. (*Parameters for the River*.)**

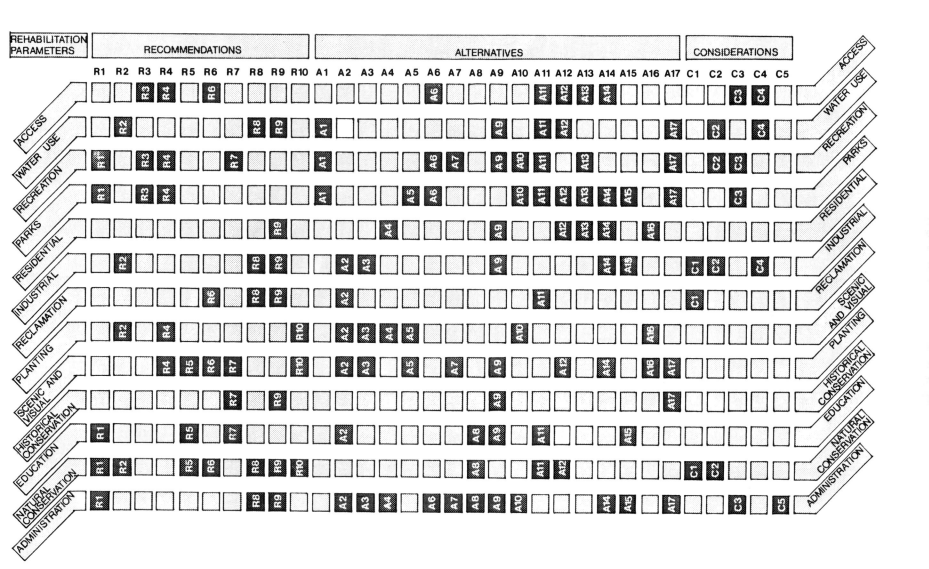

2.3   Access to foreshore and water reclaimed for
public use, with a new jetty, parking and picnic
areas. Hen and Chickens Bay, Drummoyne.

REHABILITATION PARAMETERS

Rather than provide a comprehensive listing of all the changes, the next section discusses each of the 13 'rehabilitation parameters' from the Report and any subsequent change affected within these. Following this, four specific projects are examined in more detail to establish their particular role in the rehabilitation process.

The original parameters were: administration; natural conservation; education; historical conservation; planting; scenic and visual; reclamation; industrial; residential; parks; recreation; water use; and access.

Administration

In 1984 the National Trust of Australia published a further report, *The Rehabilitation of the Parramatta River*.[2] This concluded that there was urgent need to review the administrative machinery covering the river, to overcome problems of division of authority and to simplify river management. This was in spite of several beneficial changes that had occurred since the Parameters Report. The continual problem for river-based projects is the fragmentation of responsibility between various levels of authority. The regionally-controlled Maritime Services Board (MSB) has responsibility for all matters below the high-water mark, including development, land reclamation and navigation. The relevant local councils – some eight in number – control land-based development. The

Regional Planning Authority legislates for developments, such as marinas, that straddle this boundary, while their Department of Public Buildings and Works constructs public wharfs and jetties. Water quality is monitored and controlled by the State Pollution Control Commission. Departments of Fisheries; Water, Sewerage and Drainage; Leisure, Sport and Tourism; Urban Transport Authority; the Heritage Council; National Parks and Wildlife Service – are other bodies with an interest in the river.

As a direct result of the Parameters Report, Concord Council successfully lobbied their fellow waterside councils to establish the Parramatta River Foreshores Access Committee. This non-statutory body set out to promote the river as a regional asset, in need of environmental improvement but with latent potential for greater public use for recreation, education and transport. It also hoped to rationalize planning of foreshore open space, liaise effectively with statutory bodies and gather information relevant to a Regional Environmental Plan (REP) for the river. They, like the National Trust, saw the need for an REP to reduce the unco-ordinated administration of the resources of the river.

In 1984, the Regional Department of Planning began an REP to produce planning and management guidelines for the river. This was initially seen as an updating of the Parameters Report, considering the river as a total system. Regrettably this remit was rapidly amended, and the subsequent draft

was devoted only to open space and recreation. Within these limited terms of reference it has produced some valuable specialist studies and some sensible, even far-reaching, planning guidelines.[3] It can be criticized, however, on two main grounds.

Firstly, it does not treat the river as a unified system, giving consideration to the demands of and conflicts between all the possible land uses, the natural values of the river and various interest groups. Open space and recreation cannot be seen in isolation. This weakness is carried through into the proposed administrative body, a Foreshores and Waterways Planning and Development Committee, consisting of the Department of Planning, the MSB and the waterside councils. Legislation would not be much altered as each authority would retain their previous planning responsibilities. This means that the Planning Department retains control over developments straddling the high-water mark but the local council controls the necessary land-based facilities. The new Foreshores and Waterways Committee would thus seem to have little relevance to these planning decisions.

Secondly, the REP is largely a land-based exercise, with emphasis generally on access to the river and little reference to sites accessible only to boaters. Similarly the management policies pay little attention to water-based activities and possible conflicts between different uses such as power boat racing, dinghy racing and sailboarding. It is estimated that one household in ten within the Sydney region owns a water craft of some description. Pressures for water space are bound to grow, but conflicts can be anticipated by sensible management. The MSB now has a Recreational Boating Division and is keen to play a lead role in developing boating facilities. However, it has little experience in recreational planning, and it is to be hoped that its actions can be controlled by the new Foreshores Committee. This Committee is expected to play a more creative role than merely that of development control. It is expected to promote the river as an educational, recreational and scenic resource and to co-ordinate any actions affecting the system. To achieve this, however, it will need funding, some form of permanent staffing and some political clout.

Conservation

The Parameters Report identified the high loss of wetlands which had occurred on the river, in particular of mangroves and salt marsh. Mangroves have been replanted in several areas, with varied success. There have also been cases of water-side house owners being prosecuted when they chopped down mangroves that were obstructing their views of the river.

An area of salt marsh has been established as part of the Bicentennial Park in Homebush Bay. About half of the area of this park is devoted to natural areas of mangrove, salt marsh and lagoons for waterbirds. Marked trails of boardwalks lead the visitor through these distinct habitats, and interpretation boards provide clear and useful information.

There is also a field study centre in Bicentennial Park for school parties, a visitor information centre with leaflets, and displays describing various aspects of the habitats. The concept for this park evolved from research and teaching projects undertaken at Macquarie University. The initial catalyst for these was, again, the Parameters Report.

Education

Other educational initiatives have been taken by the National Trust and by individual councils. Following publication of its report, the National Trust funded an officer to stimulate and co-ordinate the development of the river as an educational resource. Seminars and tours were held for local geography teachers to demonstrate the potential of the river in teaching environmental studies. A teacher's resource kit on mangroves was also produced. At a local level, the Environmental Officer for Concord involved schools in planting projects, and organized walks and tours related to river rehabilitation (Fig.2.4).

History

The publication of the National Estate in 1974 stimulated interest in the cultural heritage throughout Australia.[4] Heritage studies are now required for all development applications, and there is a genuine desire to retain artefacts that record the history of the nation. At least two councils have completed heritage studies, recording sites and buildings of cultural significance. The Parramatta River was thus classified in 1983 on the National Trust Register, for aesthetic and cultural

2.4 Interpretation board, picnic shelter and native planting at Bayview Park, Hen and Chickens Bay.

reasons. At site level, the former home of the poet Banjo Patterson has been restored as part of a park bearing his name, and key elements of the former animal quarantine station at Abbotsford will be retained as this becomes a local park. The regional importance of the park-like grounds of the Thomas Walker and Dame Eadith Walker hospitals has been identified in the REP and by the local council. Foreshore access has been obtained through these grounds.

Planting

The Parameters Report recommended the use of native planting, local to the Sydney area. This policy has largely been followed in the new parks and walks developing along the river. For example Concord Council are using turpentine trees (*Syncarpia glomulifera*) in a major planting exercise in Queen Elizabeth Park. This decision was based on information from the Report that the turpentine was formerly the most prevalent species in Concord, prior to wholesale clearance for development.

Scenic and visual

The Foreshores Committee tried to develop the scenic and visual policies outlined in the Parameters Report. Their lack of success was mainly due to the non-statutory basis of the group. The REP, however, has used visual assessment as the core to its planning guidelines. Its study used similar survey methods to those of the Parameters Report: recording the views from both land and water

they have subdivided the area into 13 separate landscape units. These are each seen to have their own individual character, determined largely through enclosure by landform, vegetation, bridges or buildings. The gazetted design and management guidelines are then mapped and annotated on plans of each unit. This approach is an attempt to treat each unit comprehensively, and force all councils within a landscape unit to participate in deciding future development applications. Even when these are not on their land area, it can be demonstrated that they will have a marked visual impact. By this means it is hoped to stimulate greater participation by councils in the rehabilitation of the river and to overcome understandable parochial attitudes.

Reclamation

The Maritime Services Board is the body responsible for examing land reclamation applications. There is now a general policy of no further reclamation on the Parramatta River foreshores. This was upheld in the case of an industrial company that lost part of its site for public road construction. An application to reclaim land to compensate was refused, a welcome change in attitude by the MSB, as the legacy of reclamations can be seen in sterile concrete retaining walls and blocked foreshore access. The eastern shore of Homebush Bay is a particularly striking example. Here a retaining wall runs for over 1km, backed by unattractive industrial complexes.

Industry

The Parameters Report highlighted the fact that most of the historic reasons for industry to choose a riverside location have gone, for instance water transport is now negligible, confined to the oil terminals and the naval areas. So the industry that remains, the Report argued, can release foreshore land for public access, and offer a better personal frontage to the river. The authors recommended offices, canteens and sitting areas to be sited next to the river and a co-ordinated planting policy to reduce the scale and visual intrusion of massive structures. These policies were enthusiastically accepted by Concord Council, which has set out to increase the amount of foreshore access, to ensure that redevelopment includes substantial tree planting, and to encourage a colour co-ordinated painting policy for industrial buildings. The council has used a combination of moral blackmail and its ability to delay approvals of development applications to implement its policies. It has also increased the depth of the building line relative to the foreshore from 9m (29.5ft) to 13.5m (44ft). This has succeeded to the point where prior discussions now take place to agree what river benefits the development will bring before an application is made. These are then incorporated in a landscape plan, which must be part of the development application. In fact the council now gives an annual award to the best industrial landscape project located in its area.

Residential

As industries become obsolete, pressure grows to redevelop the sites for other uses, increasingly residential. The foreshore building limits, both those in the REP and on council statutes – apply to these uses. The balance between competing uses is, however, often determined by other factors. For example, toxic materials existing on one redundant industrial site obviously rule out residential uses there, whilst at Mort Bay – an area with a long history of ship building and dock use – pressure from the local community strongly influenced the mix and form of the eventual proposals.

A major problem highlighted in the Parameters Report was the large proportion of foreshore occupied by private homes and thus denied to public use (Fig. 2.5). An interesting clause in the REP addresses this problem: future applications made for an extension to a water-front property, must include a part of their foreshore as public open space. This will apply even to minor extensions such as garages and dormer windows. It will be extremely interesting to see how this works in practice; the management implications for what initially will be isolated land-locked patches of ground are challenging. But the potential to establish informal neighbourhood launching sites for small craft and sailboards is enormous. Also, some of the totally landlocked sites could prove to be useful as short-stop destinations for boaters.

2.5 **Public access to foreshore and water prevented by private housing. Mangroves have been removed for gardens and slipways.**

Parks

Some 20 new or upgraded foreshore parks were identified by the National Trust report in 1984. These included land-fill sites, former industrial areas, and open space required as part of residential development. In addition most councils identified potential sites that would greatly enhance the riverside amenities for their communities, if and when they became available for purchase. Leichhardt Municipality, with one of the worst ratios of open space to population in the area, was particularly keen to win back under-used dockland areas, identifying a potential Bicentennial Park at Rozelle Bay.

At the same time, the Regional (State) Planning Department commissioned an extremely rapid report to encourage and assist foreshore councils with submissions for special grants, at national and regional level to fund park development. These grants were part of the Community Employment Programme (CEP) and the Sydney Green Space Programme (SGSP). Suitable projects could be entirely financed through these schemes, with 70 per cent coming from CEP, and 30 per cent from the Regional SGSP. Recognizing the regional significance of the Parramatta River, the Planning Department commissioned a further report to ensure that a co-ordinated approach was followed in the design of any foreshore parks submitted for approval by the different councils.[5]

The consultant, Land Systems of Sydney, examined some 15 sites, extending from Silverwater to Balmain East. They relied heavily on the Parameters Report for the general background and on their own on-site

assessments for their proposals. General planning and design guidelines were prepared to ensure a continuity of development standards in all sites and to avoid duplication of facilities. The standard guidelines covered vegetation, earthworks, access, water's edge, site elements, visual considerations, heritage and promotions. Site specific guidelines, in the form of written and graphic assessments of the opportunities that each site offered for park development, were also produced. The entire study was carried out in two weeks, and concluded with a meeting between council and regional officials and consultants. There was a positive response from the local officials, who, although knowledgeable about their own sites were often unaware of the wider regional factors which were frequently the major influence over choice of design options. The majority of the parks recorded in the National Trust report of 1984 resulted from these employment and green spaces initiatives (Fig. 2.6).

Recreation

Land Systems had sought where possible to link the separate foreshore parks either to each other or to adjacent open spaces. This objective was in line with the Parameters Report's views on access, which sought to make as much of the foreshore as possible available to public use. This particular parameter seems to have been pursued by most local councils and is probably the one that is now most obvious on the ground. The National Trust report identified some 55 foreshore access projects either completed or planned in 1984. There are also proposals in

2.6 Prince Edward Park, Concord, with rehabilitated public use of a foreshore, previously dominated by industry. Native trees and shrubs complement the natural outcrops of sandstone.

2.7   **Foreshore footpath giving access to the water for small boats. Hen and Chickens Bay.**

some areas to reinforce or develop pedestrian access inland, alongside existing parks and water channels. A jogging trail along the foreshore at Iron Cove also provides access for more sedentary users. Easements for a foreshore trail have been negotiated at Exile Bay across a golf course and through industrial land, to connect two foreshore parks. All councils have set foreshore building lines, ranging from 9m (29.5ft) to 50m (164ft), which will ensure that any redevelopment projects will have to provide public access along the river (Fig.2.7).

Water use and access

The Department of Public Works has provided both jetties and slipways along the river, usually in association with park developments. The major requirement for water use and access, the final two rehabilitation parameters, is for recreational boating. There is an insatiable demand for moorings and for launching ramps. A large marina has been included as part of the redevelopment of the former tyre factory at Birkenhead Point. This type of development is in line with the findings of the Parameters

Report. The original buildings have been retained and modified into a shopping centre and a maritime museum, and public access to the water regained. In some details, however, the development has not fully exploited its foreshore location: most facilities turn their back on the river, focusing on an internal mall and only one restaurant overlooks the water (Fig.2.8). There is also a proposal to site another marina just across Iron Cove, with the wharfs west of the bridge but parking on the east on the redundant power station site.

The most beneficial improvement to the river, however, is in the quality of the water.[6]

2.8 **A redundant industrial area converted to retail and commercial functions, including a marina. Birkenhead Point, Iron Cove.**

Since the Clean Water Act came into effect in 1972, the State Pollution Control Commission has been empowered to control the discharge of pollutants into the river from industry, government authorities – such as sewerage works – and private individuals. Under dry water conditions, the water quality in the river is now good. Point sources of pollution from industry and sewerage outfalls have been closed down or cleaned up. The remaining problems arise following heavy rainfall, when the city storm drains – and sometimes sewerage outfalls – cannot cope and the additional load is carried directly to the river. For two to four days following these overflows the river quality deteriorates severely. Garden and street rubbish is washed down, along with large amounts of sediment. This sediment discharge has however a beneficial side as it encourages mangrove establishment in the areas where it is deposited.

This outline of some of the results of the 13 rehabilitation parameters shows that the 1975 study has had, and continues to have, a major influence on the attitudes and perceptions of authorities and individuals towards the Parramatta River. The river is now central to the policies of foreshore councils, a magnet for recreation and a focus for redevelopment projects. The next section of this chapter describes briefly four such developments to see how the design of each has responded to the values and resources of the river. The projects are the urban redevelopment site at Mort Bay, Balmain; the foreshore access project at Exile Bay; Wangal Centennial Bush Reserve, at Mortlake Point; and the State Bicentennial Park at Homebush Bay.

MORT BAY

The Mort Bay project demonstrates the influences of heritage, the conflicts between regional and community aspirations, and the technical problems of dealing with planting on derelict industrial land. The bay is sited on the eastern end of the Balmain Peninsula, contained by a continuous, built-up ridge line from Ballast Point in the north to Simmons Point in the south. Goat Island shelters the entrance to the Bay, but there are long views over and past this to the Harbour Bridge, the North Shore and Middle Harbour.

The first dry dock in Australia was established here between 1851 and 1855. This continued in operation until the 1950s, when the site was purchased by a shipping company which infilled the dock area to create first a passenger and later a container terminal. This company ceased operation in 1975. From the time of the first dock, associated industries and cottage housing for workers developed around the bay, establishing a very distinct urban character. Later industrial buildings tended to lose this relationship, changing their materials and increasing in scale. By 1975 Mort Bay was an area of large, wide-span industrial sheds fronting a wharf area that it no longer utilized. Meanwhile the close-knit streets of nineteenth-century cottages that enclosed these sheds had been gentrified, with the original working-class owners superseded by young professionals, keen to live close to the city centre in an agreeable environment. These new residents naturally became passionately involved with the proposals to redevelop Mort Bay.

A local survey carried out in 1979 showed that 58 per cent of the community wanted the site to become a local park whilst 42 per cent preferred housing. The site was acquired by the New South Wales State Government in 1980, with a view to following, broadly, both these community requirements. At this stage another proposal was put forward to make use of the existing wharf and quay structures and to develop the area as a regional boating facility. This would have incorporated launching facilities, workshops and moorings. The local community vehemently opposed it, mainly because of the extra volume of traffic it would have caused through their steep and narrow streets. Unfortunately the argument became polarized, and a sensible compromise suggestion from the Foreshores and Access Committee to provide some low-key boat storage and launching facilities for the local residents was also opposed. Consequently the area was re-zoned for housing and public open space, and the NSW Department of Housing appointed consultants to prepare plans in 1985.

The housing is in two separate areas, to the west and the north of the bay. In total there are 210 units, for an estimated population of 525 persons. The aim is for a well-integrated mix of ages, with starter homes, family-sized units, and dwellings for retired persons. Two shops and a community centre are also provided. The urban design concept and the house types are seen to reflect both the scale and character of Balmain.

The local park consists of a strip along the waterfront extended as a finger between the two housing areas, back to the existing street pattern. The houses tend to be isolated from the park, by screen walls and topography (Fig. 2.9). The park design attempts to build on existing views. The brief was to provide foreshore open space for informal active and passive use, to encourage access to the water's edge and to interpret the cultural history of the site. These objectives were the result of discussions with the local residents carried out by community liaison consultants. Consultations with the community will continue after the project is completed, both to monitor how well the implementation meets the perceived needs of the locals and to debate and agree any adjustments required to the design over time.

The central finger of open space provides the main view and access into the park. It also contains the original dry dock, demolished and buried when the site was converted to a container terminal; the form of the dock is marked by a line of sandstone blocks which defines the paths. Views out to the bay and back to Balmain are emphasized by avenue planting. This formal planting continues along the quayside, defining the boundary between it and the informal recreation areas. These areas are grassed, and visually contained by further groups of trees. Steps give access to the water at two points, for

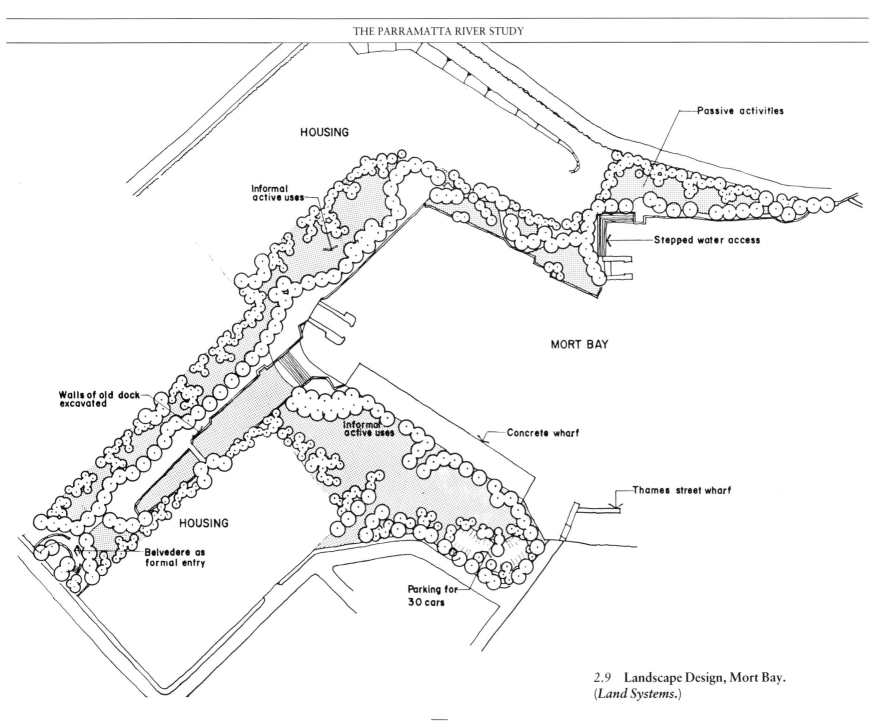

HOUSING

Passive activities

Informal
active uses

Stepped water access

MORT BAY

Walls of old dock
excavated

Informal
active uses

Concrete wharf

Thames street wharf

HOUSING

Belvedere as
formal entry

Parking for
30 cars

2.9   Landscape Design, Mort Bay.
(*Land Systems.*)

bathing. There is no formal provision for boat launching and no boat storage provided either here or in the housing areas. The original concrete wharf, however, has been retained, so although the water edge resource is not being heavily exploited at present the opportunity for future utilization has not been closed off.

Mort Bay meets several of the parameters set out in the original Parramatta River report – replacing incompatible industry with housing, opening up the foreshore to public use – in this case a length of some 700m (2,296ft) – and interpreting cultural history. The project planners also involved – and continue to involve – the local community in the planning and design process. In this case it has led to local perceptions overruling wider opportunities to develop the existing quay and wharf. Unfortunately this would seem to have polarized into an argument for either a regional scale of boating development or no such development. In the process the possibility for local residents to store and launch small portable craft has, for the meantime, been lost.

WELLCOME PHARMACEUTICALS
FORESHORE REDEVELOPMENT

The Wellcome Company owns a large industrial site on the peninsula between France and Exile Bays. The property extends to the water's edge on both bays and effectively cuts off foreshore access to Prince Edward Park, on the point of the peninsula. Concord Council, the local municipality, was keen to try and use the Parramatta River report as a planning and technical tool to rehabilitate their foreshore, and to increase access. Consequently, when Wellcome made a planning application to extend their buildings fronting onto Exile Bay, the council requested a site improvement plan as part of the submission. This plan would show how the new building and other provisions would respond positively to the river, and provide a 13.5m (44ft) wide strip of foreshore, to allow public access between the adjacent golf course and Prince Edward Park. Wellcome resisted this request, and the issue was taken to the Land Court, which ruled against them. As a result they employed a landscape consultant, who prepared and implemented a scheme that satisfied both the council and the company. Subsequently the finished design won an award for best industrial river frontage improvement scheme (Fig. 2.10). The design follows the industrial rehabilitation parameter in bringing recreation and leisure functions for the operatives to the riverside, so providing both a buffer and a connection. In the public foreshore area, new land formation up to 3m (9.5ft) high provides additional privacy and shelter. Planting also follows a parameter, by using *Casuarina sp.* along the foreshore. Mangrove rehabilitation has been attempted by the council, but with limited success. The foreshore strip was paid for and is maintained by Wellcome. The overall result is extremely successful, providing an attractive façade to the river, in contrast to previous developments that treated the river very much as a backyard. Future phases in Wellcome's development plan envisage provision of public foreshore access to their land on France Bay, connecting this also to Prince Edward Park. This project is an apt illustration of how a landscape planning document such as the Parramatta River report can be used to provide incremental rehabilitations, which over a period of time amount to major improvements.

2.10 **Integration of industry with the riverside. The factory layout now recognizes the importance of the river frontage. New public foreshore access cleverly merges with the building forecourt. Wellcome Pharmaceuticals, Hen and Chickens Bay.**

WANGAL CENTENNIAL BUSH RESERVE

Wangal Reserve is an interesting example of a scheme that has developed over a period of years, responding to various financial and planning opportunities. It was purchased by Concord Council, with considerable assistance from the State Planning Department, in 1979. Concord began rebuilding the sea-wall, on Parameter principles, using CEP finance. Later, with finance from the Sydney Green Spaces Programme, the council engaged a consultant to prepare comprehensive design proposals. A plan of management was accepted in 1983, and the project has been implemented in two stages.[7]

The park is situated on Mortlake Point, the extremity of a narrow peninsula extending from the southern river bank. To the south the peninsula was developed for industrial use, with no public foreshore access. The views from the point, however, are extensive and attractive. Access is by road through the industrial area, so the probability is that all users would come by car.

Although the site is small in area, for its size it has a long and varied water edge – beach, sandstone outcrop and concrete sea-wall. The sandstone outcrop extends as a undulating spine separating flatter areas from south to north across the site. As at Mort Bay, large areas had been in industrial use, which meant that the scheme used land reclamation techniques to establish vegetation. An existing mature Port Jackson fig (*Ficus rubiginosa*) and a screen of *Casuarina sp.* were the only existing vegetation of note (Fig.2.11).

The park design fell broadly into two parts: the flat, open area on the south-west, contrasting with a remodelled ground form in the north-east. The two are connected by a 'tunnel' walk between dense shrubs along the ridge and by a shoreline promenade. A timber jetty on the western shore provides mooring for boat-borne users, but there are no formal boat-launching facilities. One area provides for larger groups and for informal games, the other consists of a series of discrete spaces for smaller groups, with a variety of size and enclosure. This park is a good example of how to re-establish indigenous vegetation when the right opportunity arises. There was very little existing vegetation at this site but it was all native. Also the landform and exposed geology lent themselves to a design using bush planting.

The consultant's plan of management also recommended the need to monitor use of the park and to review, every five years, the management plan itself. Concord Municipality already carry out twice-yearly user surveys in their foreshore parks. These record numbers of users and the distance they have travelled; use of various facilities; demands for extra or additional facilities; seasonal variations in visitor numbers and in the use of facilities. By including Wangal in these surveys it will be possible to evaluate its popularity and performance against other foreshore parks. In addition the consultant suggests that council staff regularly monitor the conditions of the site to check on soil erosion, performance of furniture and pavings, and on whether the park is being overused or misused. Interestingly the plan of management suggested that staff performance also be monitored, to ensure that they have the necessary skills and interest to carry out their tasks effectively and efficiently.

This park is an example of two authorities anticipating changing attitudes towards the river, and winning back an area for public use well in advance of an obvious public demand. At present there is no adjacent population to use the park casually, but at weekends the car park is full and the picnic spaces crowded. It acts as a marker of future intentions for the area, when developments within the present industrial zone will be required to pay careful regard to the river and to integrate their proposed designs. The five-yearly review of the plan of management will evaluate how effective it has been in guiding the development and control of the park and to assess how it can be amended to accommodate any perceived changes in time. This is in addition to the continuous monitoring process carried out by council staff. The review should include 'an evaluation of past performance, a reassessment of the park's role and objectives, a review of the park's response to community needs, a review of administration and organisation responsibilities'. The response of the public to the management and use of the park should also be ascertained. It is

suggested that the review is undertaken by a non-council person, either someone from the State Department of Planning, or a consultant. This particular aspect of the management plan clearly recognizes that no design can ever be static. These suggestions

therefore establish a process for evaluating over a period of time the design and management performances against their original, baseline goals and to prescribe amendments that respond to any shortcomings or natural changes in demand.

2.11   A new timber jetty provides access to water over an old seawall. A flat barbecue area is enclosed by landforms and native planting. The large fig tree in the background was the only tree originally on the site. Wangal Park, Concord.

BICENTENNIAL PARK
HOMEBUSH BAY

This project is an example of educational, conservation and administrative interests combining to rehabilitate a degraded and threatened part of the river foreshore. The site is at the northern end of Homebush Bay, bisected by the canalized Powell's Creek. The wider Homebush Bay area is heavily industrialized, with chemical industries on the east bank and light and storage industries, a ship-breaking yard and an obsolete brickworks on the west. Radio masts are scattered around the edge of the bay. Road, rail and pipeline easements cross the site, and landfill operations, using both domestic waste and demolition rubble, occur in the southern area.

Homebush Bay has historically been seen as an industrial backyard and open sewer. The majority of the foreshore has been reclaimed and is edged with severe concrete sea-walls. Earlier this century the MSB established a bund of rockfill and gravel in the south-west corner of the bay as a prelude to reclaiming the area for industry. Demand for industrial expansion did not materialize, however, and the area behind the bund has evolved into two richly diverse habitats: a shallow lake, utilized by a wide variety of birds, and a salt marsh. The bunding has also encouraged new mangrove development in the bay and offered protection to the existing groves along Powell's Creek: in all, a happy environmental accident. Although the Parramatta River report recognized the value of these largely

human-induced habitats, they were still seen by some interests as wasteland with potential for development. A proposal to install an additional group of radio masts in the mangrove area was narrowly forestalled by the three municipalities of Auburn, Strathfield and Concord, whose boundaries meet at Homebush Bay.

The Parameters Report was a major factor influencing this local government decision. It had drawn the municipalities' attention to the environmental values of the area and convinced them of the desirability of rehabilitating the river as a total system, which would be of greater benefit to their ratepayers than the present industrial backyard. Concord Council was so keen to explore the environmental potential of the area that they funded a study by Macquarie University, resulting in a report, *A Bicentennial Park for Sydney*, published in 1978.[8] This study proposed a park offering 'a wide and enriching variety of recreational and aesthetic experiences . . . an appropriate character . . . evolved from existing areas by removing some of the present abuses, enhancing the remaining natural assets and ensuring that future development is designed to blend harmoniously within the framework of an overall master plan of development and management'.

In essence the Macquarie study proposed a regional park providing opportunities for nature study, informal walking and

picnicking areas, plus places for organized sports facilities. The project was to be undertaken by the NSW State Authority as a project to celebrate the 200th anniversary of the first European settlement in Australia. The report fired the imagination of the NSW planners, who re-zoned the area from industrial use to open space. Funds were provided to develop the area along Powell's Creek as a State Park, and the landscape section of the State Public Buildings and Works Department (PBWD) was commissioned to design and implement the project. Coincidentally the state also began to develop a regional sports stadium on the site proposed by the Macquarie study. The three municipalities set up an inter-council committee to co-ordinate their approach to Homebush Bay; a representative from Macquarie University serves on this committee.

The park project was elevated to a Bicentennial Project by the Office of the State Premier because they saw it as a project similar in scope and concept to the Centennial Park created in eastern Sydney in 1888. More funds were provided and the project was accelerated to be completed for the 1988 deadline. Conceptually the PBWD Bicentennial Park was along similar lines to the initial Macquarie proposal. The detail design, particularly in the informal recreation areas, was, however, quite different (Fig.2.12).

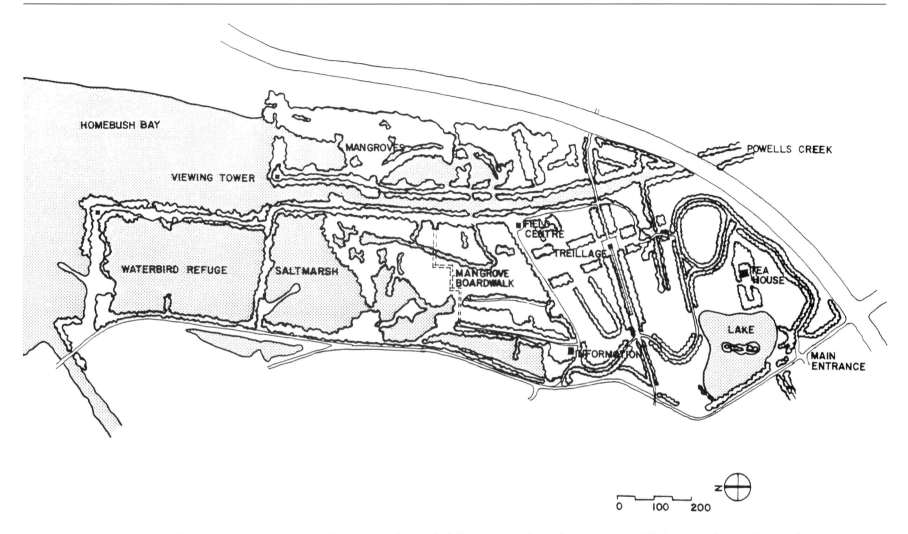

HOMEBUSH BAY

MANGROVES

POWELLS CREEK

VIEWING TOWER

FIELD CENTRE

TREILLAGE

WATERBIRD REFUGE

SALTMARSH

MANGROVE BOARDWALK

TEA HOUSE

LAKE

INFORMATION

MAIN ENTRANCE

0   100   200

2.12 A plan of Bicentennial Park, Homebush Bay.

In essence the park falls into two broad areas: the 'natural' zone of mangrove, saltmarsh and lake; and the parkland on the reclaimed rubbish tips. Surface-water drainage patterns, service easements and pedestrian circulation have heavily influenced the parkland design. In some cases what would seem to be minor constraints have been

magnified to justify key design decisions. On the other hand important technical and environmental aspects sometimes appear to have been sidestepped. For example, the major design axis of the canal and promenade was justified by the pedestrian connection across the park, between the West Concord railway station and a technology park. The regular use of this, a walk of some twenty minutes in duration, is hard to envisage. On the technical side little attention seems to have been paid to the techniques required for planting on land-fill sites. Methane drains have been provided for the built structures, such as restaurants and pavilions, and these are constructed on rafts to anticipate settlement. But the draft management plan has no references to problems arising from methane gas leakage in planted areas. Construction techniques used for the paths and canal are very poor and are unlikely to withstand heavy, sustained use. In major parts, the site appears to have been manipulated to meet the demands of a preconceived formalistic design.

The natural area of the park, however, is extremely successful, apart from a lack of accommodation in the field study centre. In particular the floating board walks through the mangroves provide both an educational and an aesthetic experience (Fig. 2.13). The formal placing of viewing towers, which act as eye-catchers and orientation markers, also works well.

In management terms, the park is run by a board of trustees, one of whom is the

2.13 Floating boardwalks provide access to the tidal mangrove flats for the public and educational groups.

landscape architect responsible for the design and implementation of the project. The trust comprises eight persons, six representing state and local government and business interests, plus the park designer and manager. Revenue funding is provided by the State Department of Environment, but park staff are part of the State National Parks and Wildlife Services. There are 16 full-time management staff, covering horticulture, general maintenance and visitor interpretation.

A plan of management is in preparation. This breaks the park into 14 zones, such as mangroves, saltmarsh, parklands and lake. Each zone is further subdivided into units, or tasks. The lake zone, for example, comprises ten units, ranging from general objectives such as recreational use to specific instructions such as reed-growth management. The management plan is more a statement of design objectives than a prescription of management and horticultural techniques by which they can be achieved, an approach which seems to fit this particular case, where both designer and manager have a continuing interest and input into the evolution of the park. However, it would probably be sensible at some stage to balance the design criteria with a manual of specific management principles and techniques. Personnel are not static within an organization, and it is wise to have some record of past working methods to ensure that future staff are fully informed of the reasons behind certain management techniques, and have a baseline against which to rationalize any changes they may wish to make. It is important that any management policy is seen as a guide, not a rigid straight-

jacket. Regular monitoring and reassessment both of principles and techniques must be undertaken. The draft management plan recognizes this as its own primary justification.

Bicentennial Park was directly influenced by the Parramatta River report. It fulfils the broad parameter of re-establishing the values of the river as a system in the regard it gives to conserving and enhancing the riverside habitats, particularly mangrove and saltmarsh. The parameter of education is met very fully by the schools programmes organized through the field study centre, by leaflets and static interpretation boards. Recreation is a prime provision, concentrating, as the Parameters Report suggests, on informal aspects. The planting, except around obviously introduced artefacts, uses local material, even in the formal areas.

The part played by the various levels of administration or authorities in the development of Bicentennial Park, and the ripple effects this has had in the wider Homebush Bay area, is particularly interesting. The State Department of Planning has produced a plan of management for the areas adjoining the park, as guidelines for the three local authorities. On the western edge, the state sports centre has been the catalyst for the re-siting of other sporting facilities, such as the trotting stadium and showgrounds. Administrators have realized that this previously disregarded area is now well serviced by freeways, railways and, potentially, a ferry. It lies close to the geographical centre of the suburban sprawl which Sydney is today, and so can attract, and accommodate, the movement of mass

audiences attracted by regional and national events. This was the location chosen for an unsuccessful bid for the 1996 Olympic Games. The publicity it generated, however, has brought the potential of the area to the attention of a wide range of interests. Although the Olympic project foundered, there would seem to be sufficient impetus to ensure a continuing rehabilitation of this previously neglected area.

The four project studies described above have attempted to demonstrate some of the developments and changes that have occurred along the foreshore, to varying degrees sparked by the Parramatta River report, and conforming to the values it set out. None of these is finite, each is planned or designed to be flexible, to accommodate change in use or in form. They are also a stimulus for other riverside changes and rehabilitation, and show that the perception of the river, in the past 15 years, has been turned around. From being an unconsidered, disregarded, degraded element, the river is now valued as a holistic system, with economic, transport, recreational and educational benefits to both the adjacent community and the wider metropolitan area (Fig. 2.14).

The Parramatta River report has played a crucial role in this reversal. It was a baseline report, establishing the condition of the natural system, setting values, and defining issues to guide the rehabilitation of the river. The authors of the report implemented no physical projects in the study area but their influence pervades the changes that have taken place since publication. The landscape plan has established rehabilitation principles, changed perceptions and, more importantly,

2.14 **Boat launching facilities at Bayview Park. Across the bay, new foreshore access at Wellcome Pharmaceuticals (left) provides a footpath between Prince Edward Park (right) and Massey Park golf course.**

generated the interest of decision makers. This flexible, interpretative approach to landscape planning would appear to have been a major factor in the rebirth of the Parramatta River.

3

Urban regeneration

The Glasgow Eastern Area Renewal Project

INTRODUCTION

The Glasgow Eastern Area Renewal Project (GEAR) was set up in May 1976, as an enabling group to tackle the economic, social and environmental problems in the area. These problems of falling population, rising unemployment and increasing urban dereliction are common to most British and indeed West European nineteenth-century industrial cities. The six communities within GEAR were originally separate villages, dependent on coal mining and textile manufacturing. The nineteenth-century expansion of Glasgow, however, encroached on their green fields in the form of dense tenement housing, brickworks, iron foundries, distilleries and ceramic and textile works. The coal mines at Shettleston fed the Parkhead forge, as this grew to be the largest single employer in Glasgow.

By 1976 much of this development was in need of renewal. The majority of housing did not meet modern standards and factories were empty, uneconomic or sources of pollution. Previous urban policies of comprehensive clearance had left either empty sites or blighted, rundown property. As a result the population had declined from 145,000 to 41,000 in 30 years. Male unemployment stood at 21 per cent, compared with 14 per cent in Glasgow as a whole. The population structure was heavily biased towards the elderly, the handicapped, the unemployed and people with lower-than-average educational attainment.[1]

GEAR was made up from agencies already operating within the area and attempted to co-ordinate their actions in order to increase their effectiveness. One agency might agree to bring forward a particular part of their programme in order to take advantage of an opportunity set up by another agency. For example the Education Department might give a commitment to build a school, or extend an existing one, to complement a housing programme – either new private developments or renovation of publicly-owned stock. A flexible approach to deciding programmes and priorities was a vital element of the project.

The main agencies contributing to GEAR were the Scottish Development Agency (SDA); the Scottish Development Department; Strathclyde Regional Council; Glasgow District Council; the Scottish Special Housing Association; and the Regional Health Board. The major funding came from the SDA, but all agencies retained their separate statutory roles. GEAR was seen more as an enabling group, a forum for discussion where a pooling of ideas and co-ordination of previously individual acts could target particular problems. The total amount spent by all agencies in GEAR between 1977 and 1986 was in excess of £315 million. The SDA contributed some £63.5 million of this. Between 1975 and 1985 the SDA spent some

£12.5 million on environmental improvement within GEAR. Together with the local and regional authorities it spent a further £7.5 million on leisure and recreation projects. The annual cost to the SDA of maintaining open space in GEAR was £400,000 in 1982–3, illustrating the need to provide continuing revenue budgets to support the initial one-off capital expenditure.

The SDA acted as client for these environmental improvement projects. The projects were run by outside professional consultants, from feasibility exercises through to supervision, construction and maintenance contracts. The Agency used their own professional staff to define the brief and budget for each project and engage and work with the consultants. As projects were related to an annual budget, a long-term programme was difficult to set or follow. For example, the Crown Point Sports Centre project required some ten separate contracts to complete.

3.1 **Existing and proposed land uses, GEAR project.** (*SDA.*)

STRATEGY

GEAR operated within existing statutory frameworks. It brought together representatives from the agencies involved to look at the particular problems of the area and to see how these could be resolved by co-ordinating, integrating and adjusting the various programmes. It was a tactical, rather than strategic, approach, with elements of trading and bargaining between agencies, and with investors. 'Networking', 'entrepreneurial', 'brokering', 'animateur' have all been used to describe this approach, where the aim was to increase the investment value of each project by a combination of land swapping, ground consolidation, infrastructure provision, investment grants and environmental improvement.

In the initial phase the Project Team tended to follow a more classical planning approach and published a Master Plan in October 1981 (Fig. 3.1). This largely responded to projects and policies already in the pipeline. In addition to locating and categorizing existing and planned areas of housing, industry and commerce, public facilities and recreation and open space, it identified areas with development potential. These fell into either 'core' or 'peripheral' areas. The six core areas were based on the urban centres, either linear in pattern, such as Shettleston or Tollcross, or nodal such as Bridgeton Cross or Parkhead. The eight peripheral areas were mainly old industrial sites such as the Cambuslang steel works site.

Environmental projects during this phase were regarded as a method of upgrading the visual and physical character of the area, both to attract investment and to raise the expectations of local people. Housing rehabilitation was seen as an immediate and visible way of rapidly improving the area. This began at both ends of the project, with a major restructuring programme in Calton, and tenement renovation in Shettleston and

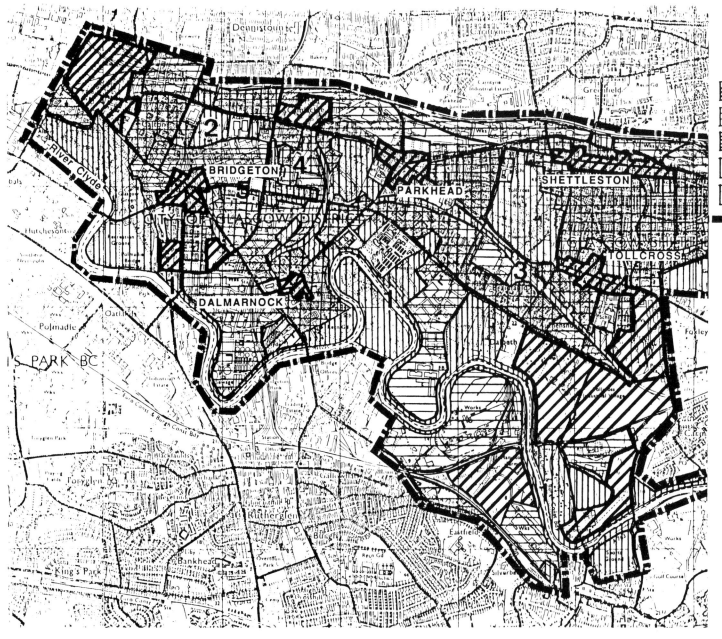

Development potential

Housing

Industry & commerce

Recreation & open space

Public facilities

GEAR boundary

1. Clyde walkway

2. Crown Point

3. Parkhead rail line

4. Barrowfield

5. London Road

3.2 *(Left)* **Much of the Calton development area has been rebuilt by the Scottish Special Housing Association (now Scottish Homes).**

3.3 *(Right)* **This raised screen of planting helps unify the major traffic route through the GEAR area; it also gives privacy to the housing areas behind London Road.**

Tollcross. Calton was largely undertaken by the Scottish Special Housing Association (SSHA), whilst tenements were improved through Housing Associations (Fig. 3.2).

Two other important projects implemented at this early stage were the Clyde Walkway and the London Road corridor improvement. Both these projects had been initiated by Glasgow District, but their implementation was made possible by the GEAR team, with capital from the SDA. Both were seen as offering immediate improvement to the area, potentially attractive to both investors and residents. The London Road scheme aimed to provide a unified and high-quality approach through the area on the main arterial route from the south. Co-ordinated paving, walling and planting created a coherent and urbane character and screened discordant housing and industrial areas. At the same time derelict areas were treated by temporary grassing and planting, and additional recreational and open-space facilities were provided for the housing areas.

The planting and construction had to be robust enough to withstand the regular foot traffic of Celtic football supporters moving to and from the city centre. By channelling fans alongside the road, by means of retaining walls and embankments, shortcutting through the housing and consequent litter and vandalism are minimized (Fig.3.3).

As projects materialized on the ground it became apparent that the classical planning approach of following a predetermined programme was not appropriate, and more flexible, managerial techniques evolved. Projects could be initiated by investor interest, site potential or a contributing agency policy.

Their final form, however, was often determined by an overlaying and evaluation of all these needs, demands and contributions. Agencies were seeking more obvious benefits from their investment – be they in the form of capital or revenue grants – in facilities, infrastructure or manpower. In this tactical approach, landscape planning became a means to an end and no longer an end in itself; it was seen instead as an integrated part of the development package, which itself was increasingly a combination of private and public finance and benefits.

It is interesting to contrast the approach taken by GEAR, in the development of the old Parkhead Railway line, between their initial feasibility study (1978) and the final form of the project. The first study set out to retain the linear pattern of the derelict railway and establish a footpath and associated open spaces – a sensible response to the existing character of the artefact. However, when the project reached contract stage (1986) under a different consultant, the decision was taken to ignore the line as an individual, continuous element, and rather to integrate it with the surrounding land-uses and communications. This involved infilling the railway cuttings using the embankments, and largely re-establishing the landforms that existed prior to the railway. There were several reasons why this approach was followed (and these will be discussed in more detail later), but the main factor was the change in attitude by the GEAR members. The site had to be marketable in land parcels to potential investors – for housing and industry – and only residual, undevelopable areas would be left as public open space.

This added-value concept towards site preparation is now followed in all projects. The role of the landscape architect is geared to preparing the land for marketing and development, not treating it as a completed project in itself. This preparation can involve land consolidation to overcome subsidence problems, removing toxic wastes, setting site levels and establishing structure planting. GEAR would expect to recoup these development costs through the added value of the land, and the capital investment by the developer. By the end of the initial ten years of GEAR's life the perception of the environmental problems had changed somewhat. In 1976, the visual and physical impression of the area was of run-down housing and derelict industry. By 1986 the physical fabric had been so turned around that the few remaining untreated sites stood out as alien elements. The major emphasis has therefore shifted from environmental improvement to one of attracting investment to attempt to increase employment.

The contribution of landscape design is obvious everywhere in the improved housing areas, the new industrial sites, the recreational facilities and the improved townscapes at Bridgeton Cross and Calton. At Bridgeton Cross a combination of traffic management and environmental improvement have recreated a focus for the neighbourhood. The Cross area has been pedestrianized, the existing Victorian shelter and clock repainted and new planting and seats provided (see Fig. 1.9).

LANDSCAPE DESIGN

The policy of GEAR is to employ private consultants, largely commissioned through the SDA. Many different landscape architects have been employed by the Agency, carrying out projects from the feasibility stage through contract to maintenance. Given this multiplicity of designers and a loose approach to co-ordinated planning, one would expect a wide and perhaps discordant variety of landscape design approaches. Although this is true at the detailed level, there is a sense of continuity, partly because of the use of structure planting and partly through colour co-ordination of fencing and trip rails to public streets. These elements and their bright red colour have almost become a symbol of GEAR, as they reappear in housing, recreational and industrial projects.

The structure planting has been restricted in all cases by cost and difficult planting conditions. Invariably the growing conditions are poor, being on either made up or severely-compacted ground. Topsoil had to be imported, and is often of dubious quality. Also there are the inevitable problems associated with establishing planting in urban areas: wilful and unintentional abuse by people and domestic pets, litter accumulation and increased wind speeds and turbulence around buildings and on street corners. Only a limited range of trees and shrubs can thrive in these conditions, so it is hardly surprising that they recur throughout the various projects by different designers. In the summer months this verdant structure planting makes a strong impression, softening the built environment, articulating the main access routes and screening undeveloped sites. It also, largely through the tree planting, gives a continuity to the area, unifying visually discordant artefacts and giving a character and setting to this distinctly urban area. Much of this plant material is fast-growing and deciduous, such as *Salix sp, Alnus glutinosa, Rosa rugosa* and *Corylus avellana*. In summer it fulfils its structural function well, but once the leaves fall the impression is much weaker, less solid and often lacking in visual interest.

In terms of detail some of the early GEAR projects have proved unsatisfactory, particularly play areas and informal recreation areas. Some consultants commendably felt it was important to provide facilities of the highest quality, with strongly-modelled land forms, much use of brick retaining walls and pavements, and sophisticated play equipment. Failure to meet these standards was due to several factors, one of which was lack of adequate supervision by qualified play leaders. Less obviously, the early projects were designed in isolation from other improvements and developments in the immediate locality – partly to put something on the ground to demonstrate physically that GEAR was active in each district, and partly to meet annual, non-recurring SDA budgets. The lack of an overall programme, particularly at local level, led to facilities being poorly located for the intended users and isolated from main circulation routes that would have given casual supervision. As a result several early

projects were severely abused, and two in particular are having to be redesigned and rebuilt.

The GEAR team have paid particular attention to the establishment and maintenance of the planting. Contracts traditionally follow a pattern of one-year site maintenance by the contractor, prior to hand over of the completed and supposedly established site to the client authority for continuing maintenance. This practice was, however, modified in two significant ways by GEAR.

Firstly, an additional two-year establishment contract was added to the initial one-year maintenance period. This contract was tendered for competitively and did not necessarily go to the original contractor. The reasoning behind this was that from observation of early GEAR projects it was clear that plants were struggling to become established in the poor growing conditions prevalent on most sites. The additional capital necessary to provide the horticultural skills to carry out such a contract could not be met by the Local Authority from their budget. So to protect their initial investment the SDA agreed to fund these two-year establishment contracts. These have proved successful and are now standard practice for all SDA projects throughout Scotland. This means that all projects are closely maintained and cultivated for three years subsequent to initial planting.

The second change to the original contract procedure was a further delay in handover to the authority with ultimate maintenance responsibility – in this case the Parks and Recreation Department of Glasgow District.

In common with all local authorities, Glasgow was experiencing severe restrictions in its annual spending budgets. To meet these, cut-backs in staff and services were made; the Parks Department did not escape its share of these. Over the same period, due to increasing land reclamation and improvement projects throughout the City, the Department was receiving considerable new areas of open space to look after. The strain on the Department was obvious, and several such projects deteriorated rapidly after handover, due to inadequate maintenance. To avoid this occurring to schemes within the GEAR areas, and also to ensure a uniform quality in their management, it was decided that all new public projects would be looked after and funded by GEAR for a further three years. Two special contracts were drawn up to cover these sites, each supervised by a Landscape Consultant.

Prior to handing over the maintenance of public sites to the Parks Department, the SDA funded a report on how the maintenance could be most efficiently carried out. This study (by Val Kripp) worked within the current budgetary, manpower and machinery levels of the Parks Department.[2] By suggesting slight amendments to existing practices his report was able to demonstrate that the Department had the capacity to manage and maintain these areas to a high standard within their available budget.

The report looked at the problems of litter, site safety and general cost effectiveness of maintenance by both the District (Public) Parks Department and the private contractors employed under the GEAR maintenance contracts. It also looked at tree management and at ways to improve the efficiency of grass cutting.

The report observed that a disturbing number of trees were leaning or falling over, particularly *Populus sp.*, due to poor, often wet, soil that led to a poorly-developed root structure. In the majority of planting blocks, fast-growing nurse or pioneer species were in need of replacement or thinning. Few of the longer-lived hardwood species included in the original planting mixtures were surviving. There was a need to thin out and coppice the pioneers and to plant additional climax species.

The report also studied three aspects of amenity grass management and was able to suggest potential savings by amending some of the establishment and maintenance contracts. These suggestions covered the application of chemical retardants to control the rate of grass growth; the use of low-maintenance grass mixes; and increasing the height of grass sward cut.

The commissioning and application of this particular study is a good illustration of how the various agencies contributing to GEAR support and help each other to ensure the success of projects. Here the SDA has been able to fund an outside study of a Local Authority Department, and this in turn has enabled that Department to adjust some of its procedures which allow it economically to take on additional tasks and so ensure the continuing quality of the external environment.

The previous sections have attempted to give a general view of how GEAR functions and the roles of landscape planning and design within the programme. To illustrate these roles, it is proposed to look at four particular projects, and discuss their procedures in some detail. The projects are the River Clyde Walkway, an example of a linear feature utilizing a natural element and connecting the East End to the city centre and the suburbs; the Parkhead rail line, which in contrast to the Clyde project destroys the linear quality of the feature to integrate it with the surrounding land-uses; Crown Point Sports area, which provides high-quality games facilities on former waste land; and the Barrowfield Community Project, a scheme that involves the local people in both improving the environment of their estate and seeking investment and employment opportunities.

RIVER CLYDE WALKWAY

This project was one of several proposals put forward in the River Clyde Study carried out in 1979.[3] The local consultants, Gillespies, looked at the river corridor from the city centre to the city boundary. The main proposals, and subsequent implementation, were concentrated within the GEAR area.

The study set out two main objectives – to prepare a planning and landscape strategy for the river corridor, including proposals for recreational use; and to make detailed and practical suggestions for rehabilitation projects arising from this strategic framework. While factors such as topography, water quality and habitat diversity were recognized, the study was based largely on a visual survey considering three categories; zones of character; structure; and envelopes. The visual character aspect covered the range, quality and general appearance of the land uses within the corridor. Visual structure recorded enclosure, by landforms, buildings or vegetation, and located viewpoints. Visual envelopes described the sphere of influence of each land use. A synthesis of these three basic surveys classified sites within the river corridor as having problems or opportunities. The sites were then analysed against five possible development strategies in order to arrive at their best use. The strategies were housing; industry; recreation; facilities for the community; and transport. The main riverside proposals were then mapped and presented to the client.

The study clearly identified the need to develop a continuous walkway along the north bank of the river. Thus a forgotten backwater would be used as the catalyst to regenerate housing, industry and recreation, by establishing a linear focus to which new and rehabilitated projects could relate. The

3.4   Clyde Walkway. Timber platforms for fishermen also provide a glimpse downriver towards the Gorbals. Native riparian planting has rapidly established to give a mature, rural quality to the river edge. The factory wall, on the right, has been repaired and painted.

walkway would provide an overall environmental framework plan and establish guidelines for riverside development. It would act as an extension of Glasgow's linear park system, and would provide links to major development sites along the corridor and outwards to adjacent communities.

The walkway proposal was subsequently carried through, in two separate contracts: the first from Shawfield Bridge to Dalmarnock; the second from there to the Cambuslang Recovery site. Gillespies were again the landscape architects. Treatment was in both cases simple and robust. Regrading

was kept to a minimum, such as locations where banks were unstable, or where access was provided to the river.

In general the path runs about 5m (16.5ft) above the water level. This posed problems both of safety and of controlled access. The walkway is fenced at connections with bridges or paths linking it to adjacent developments, and where it passes alongside residential areas. The fence is of strong, tubular, mild steel, painted dark brown. Seats and litter bins are in chunky timber sections, which are generally wearing well. Connection to the river was provided either visually in the

form of timber platforms extending the footpath above the riverbank at key points or by timber steps and boardwalks. These leave the main footpath and descend gradually to water level, where they widen into fishing platforms (Fig. 3.4). The footpath is surfaced with a self-binding, buff-coloured gravel, except at entry points such as bridges. Here, where more intense wear is anticipated, granite setts or asphalt are used. The character is pleasantly informal.

This informality is also picked up by the planting, with the exception of the stretch next to the Dalmarnock high-rise flats. Here the native shrubs have been individually clipped and isolated in areas of mown grass. The abrupt change in character is emphasized by the natural treatment of the adjacent riverbank vegetation. Much of the north bank was barren and lacking in vegetation. The planning study had called for large-scale tree planting to improve the visual environment, to screen and reduce the apparent scale of derelict areas and to stabilize banks. The planting carried out in the first phase (Shawfield Bridge-Dalmarnock) aimed to achieve this by using a mixture of hardy plants that occur within the Clyde Valley. These were intended to give a coherence throughout the length of the walkway and provide a background for other plants used to add interest, provide emphasis or act as a screen. The majority of the framework planting consisted of fast-growing species, well adapted to wet sites with poor soil conditions, including typical land reclamation species such as *Alnus glutinosa*, *Salix alba* and

S. caprea. A small percentage of longer-lived species, such as oak and ash, were planted. Shrubs were planted at the density of five plants to the square metre (11 sq. ft) to ensure rapid cover and consequent weed suppression. Plants were directly notch planted into the river bank with little or no ground preparation. In contrast, areas across the path were cultivated and some topsoil was imported.

This first stage of the walkway was completed in 1980. It was managed under the standard GEAR establishment and maintenance contracts and has now been handed over to Glasgow District Parks Department. In many instances the planting has been too successful, encroaching onto the path and blocking river views from specially designed sitting areas. During the summer open parts of the river bank are covered in dense herbaceous species, dominated by the exotic Himalayan Balsam (*Impatiens glandulifera*). There is little sign of wilful

damage to the planting. As with much planting in the GEAR area it is rather dominated by pioneer species and is also lacking in evergreen components.

The walkway does seem to have achieved one of the objectives in the planning study: that of creating links between the river and adjacent areas – both housing and industry. It also appears to function well as an alternative pedestrian route between communities. As a catalyst to encourage development on adjacent sites, however, the Clyde Walkway would appear to have been less successful. There are few signs of new housing or industrial units, and the peripheral area is rather nebulous in character. This may be due partly to uncertainty in areas safeguarded for a proposed, and indefinitely postponed, inner ring road. Nevertheless, when the SDA next instigated a linear project – the Parkhead rail line – the brief to the designer had a different slant to that of the Clyde Study.

PARKHEAD RAIL LINE

This project aimed to rehabilitate the derelict Parkhead rail line, from the eastern boundary of the GEAR area to the Celtic football stadium. At this latter point the line enters a tunnel that needs occasional maintenance by British Rail engineers. A study of the line was undertaken in 1977, which proposed retaining the linear character as a walkway. Only the most easterly part was implemented at this time, where a cutting and adjacent land

were planted under a community programme. This was supervised by a local conservation group, using native species, with the aim of developing the site for environmental education.

When the SDA reconsidered treatment of the Parkhead line in 1985, the solution agreed on was radically different. This was for two main reasons. Firstly, the local residents were strongly against the proposal to develop the

line as a pedestrian way since it was used as an escape route by burglars and the cuttings as dens for glue sniffers. They felt an official route would not stop these activities and would also attract boisterous football supporters travelling to and from Celtic Park. The other reason was that the SDA had changed their approach towards funding environmental improvements. Such improvements could now receive funding only if they were part of a package that improved the development potential of the site. In other words, the investment in the site had to be seen to increase its market value.

The 1985 proposals for the line therefore demonstrated a totally new approach to that of the earlier study. Basically it was to be reintegrated with the local topography and land uses. Embankments were used to infill cuttings, and land parcels were incorporated into private housing sites, added as either carparks to an existing sports facility or expansion space to existing industrial or manufacturing areas. Only where land was unbuildable, because of either instability due to old mine works or inaccessibility, was it developed as open space (Fig. 3.5). Here, the treatment of each site varied: permanent sites adjacent to existing housing were designed to meet the needs of the residents and require a high level of maintenance; landlocked sites with no development potential were planted out with trees and shrubs. As an experiment, one area was tree-seeded in contrast to the usual small whips and transplants. One site

that may have future development potential has merely been put down to grass.

Treatment throughout has been straightforward and sensible. The sites added to existing industry have been regraded, planted with screening trees – usually as advanced nursery stock – and fenced (Fig. 3.6). Sites for housing have been regraded and seeded with grass.

So in contrast to the Clyde Walkway, the linear unity of the railway has deliberately been destroyed. Rather than one uniformly-treated scheme, the Parkhead line has been designed as discrete packages, relating to the areas perpendicular to the line. Visually, the old line will disappear and become reabsorbed into the urban grain, relating once more to the local road and land-use scales and patterns. At the same time, two existing industrial units remain and have expanded, two sites for private housing have been created, useful open space has been provided for local residents and the parking problems associated with a sports complex have been solved.

3.5 *(Opposite)* **The Parkhead railway has been altered and planted to create an informal open space, shared by housing areas previously separated by the rail line.**

3.6 *(Page 63)* **The railway embankment has been partly regraded to extend an existing industrial yard. Planting on the remaining slopes provides screening for adjacent houses.**

CROWN POINT SPORTS CENTRE

This project was carried out as a series of rolling contracts between 1980 and 1984. The site, some 16.5 ha (41 acres) in extent, was an area of derelict and semi-demolished tenements and workshops, the central part of an urban block. To the west two new housing areas sandwich the old Victorian school of St Mary's. The more recent schools of St Anne's

and St Mungo's are on the east, and an isolated post office building sits on the southern boundary. The site was initially a joint venture between Strathclyde Region, Glasgow District and the SDA.

The brief to the designers, ASH, was to provide an all-weather athletics track, three all-weather football pitches, a grass rugby

pitch, car parking and a service yard. Later two further pitches were added at St Mary's and St Anne's schools. Floodlighting was required for the running track and one of the all-weather pitches.

Given the form of the site and the strict requirements of the brief, the layout developed as a simple range of north-south oriented pitches, with the running track next to St Mungo's. There are three entrances: from the south vehicles and pedestrians arrive at the main building; an embankment screens the running track, which is reached through the main building; and the northern entrance,

off the Gallowgate, leads to a formal pedestrian avenue between the rugby pitch and the track. An entrance also brings pedestrians from the west, where a mound, made up from site rubble, breaks up the inevitable horizontality of the pitches and provides an overview of the site (Fig.3.7). The site is further subdivided spatially, as the rugby pitch and athletics track are raised some 2m (6½ft) above the all-weather pitches to the south. This was to minimize expensive excavations into the stone basements and foundations of the old tenements. Instead these were infilled and levelled off with

3.7 (Left) **Running track and football pitches at the Crown Point Sports Centre are separated by earth mounding and stone retaining walls.**

3.8 (Right) **Grass rugby pitches at Crown Point Sports Centre.**

imported subsoil before the finished surfaces were applied.

The Regional Education Department envisaged the facilities as being shared by the pupils of St Mungo's, with the school's indoor facilities being available for public use in evenings and holidays. Due to management problems this has not happened, however, and the corridor linking the Sports Centre to the school has been bricked off and never used. This means that the facilities provided at Crown Point are not as varied as originally anticipated. The only internal amenities are a small gym, changing rooms, restaurant and facilities for judges and spectators.

In a sports area where defined functions and spaces so clearly relate, the role of planting is essentially one of reinforcing the spatial definition. At Crown Point, earth mounding around the north and west of the site has been heavily planted with trees and shrubs. Trees also articulate the southern boundary, but without the initial elevation given by mounding. There is additional planting at the entrance areas, both pedestrian and vehicular. Here trees such as *Sorbus aria*, *S. aucuparia* and *Alnus glutinosa* are underplanted with a range of shrubs and ground covers.

Crown Point Sports Centre was not open to the public until all the work was completed. This was carried out under a rolling series of some ten contracts, mainly to fit in with the SDA budget constraints. The early planting therefore had an opportunity to settle in and become established before being exposed to normal wear and tear. In contrast to other projects discussed, this site has been managed by the Parks Department since contract handover. The area is fenced and semi-protected, the users are there for a purpose, and the Parks Department manage this as a flagship site with three full-time operatives on maintenance. Consequently the project looks healthy, the planting is growing well and the site is kept neat and tidy (Fig. 3.8).

BARROWFIELD ENVIRONMENTAL PROJECT

The Barrowfield housing estate lies on the northern edge of the GEAR area. It is bounded on the north and south by main traffic routes: Gallowgate and London Road. Celtic Park football stadium lies on the eastern edge, with warehousing and industrial units on the west. The estate consists of 614 flats, in the form of three- or four-storey blocks, all with stair access. At the time the Project began the population was approximately 2000, and there was a male unemployment rate of some 50 per cent.

There was a feeling that the estate had been by-passed in the general environmental improvement of GEAR, and the residents felt they were missing out on the apparent new prosperity around them. One reason for this was that the housing blocks had been improved in the early 1970s, with new pitched roofs replacing the original flat ones. However, both the internal and external environments rapidly deteriorated, due partly to poor design and management.

By the early 1980s, the general GEAR policy had moved from one of investment in environmental improvement *per se* to one of seeking projects where investment would create employment opportunities for local people. The SDA, who were the main funding agency for environmental improvement, now realized that their investment in tidying and greening formerly derelict areas had not noticeably attracted investment that offered local employment. The majority of new development had been either housing or small businesses relocating from outwith GEAR, thus bringing in non-GEAR-based employees. The master plan for the Barrowfield Environmental Project, produced in late 1984, aimed to use investment in environmental improvements positively to create local employment and stimulate small locally-based businesses.[4] The project defined four stages to achieve this community, environment-led, employment: the so-called Barrowfield System-Strategy; Preliminary Groundwork; Managing the Project; and Running the Project.

The strategy was based on the premise that there was already a large sum of money being invested in Barrowfield, mainly by the Housing Authority, in the form of repairs, maintenance and security. Capital funds for improvements would also come from the SDA and the Glasgow District Council. If this money could be channelled into local initiatives, in addition to the prime function of improvement, jobs for local people would also be created. The responsibility for developing suitable projects and allocating the funds to them would be largely shared between a locally-based community worker and the project co-ordinator, in this case a landscape consultant (Cunning Young & Associates). The strategy spelt out the need to develop confidence in and commitment to the project from both the community and the funding and housing authorities. Local Authority rules and standing orders would need to be amended in order to achieve the employment and training goals whilst at the same time maintaining standards of workmanship and security.

This community development approach was also applied by the Social and Welfare Services. A local manager was established within the Neighbourhood or Community Centre to ensure that residents could obtain advice and support from within the community. This covered help with claiming welfare benefits and payments for outstanding bills. The Local Authority also seconded a Community Development Officer to advise the Community Business Company on training and further education opportunities. This enabled residents to learn skills that could get them back into employment.

The 'preliminary groundwork' gathered the information needed to produce an acceptable master plan. The study was in two parts: a physical record and appraisal of the area, and a public participation exercise to make contact with the local people and to obtain their perceptions of the problems. These turned out to be mainly non-visual, relating instead to aspects of traffic circulation, security and refuse collection. In an area so lacking in basic amenities, it is hardly surprising that the residents rank environmental quality so low. House-to-house interviews were conducted, and the proposals were taken back for examination and discussion at public and community meetings as the master plan evolved.

The master plan, the end result of the 'groundwork' stage, integrated all the proposals into detailed plans and costed programmes for each phase. The links built up during this process between the design, or rather enabling, consultant, the authorities and the community, clearly contributed to the success of the project on the ground during the subsequent 'project management' and 'running' stages.

Three groups were formed to facilitate the management: a consultative body, acting as a Board of Directors, and consisting of tenants, contributing authorities and local businesses; a management consultant (the landscape architect) to co-ordinate and manage the project from inception to completion; and a management contractor, to co-ordinate the implementation of the project. Both consultant and contractor were to ensure a high level of senior- or partner-level commitment to the project, individuals whom the residents could readily identify and relate to as the work progressed. The contractor was also legally committed to employing a fixed percentage of locals on his permanent payroll, and to provide them with skills training. They would also sub-contract work to local Barrowfield Community businesses as these became established. The contractor was selected by interview, not competitive tendering, to ensure a commitment to the overall concept of the Barrowfield project.

Three basic and interrelated requirements were identified for successfully running the project. These were full tenant participation, total security for the work both in progress and when completed, and a more positive role for housing management. Thus locals are now involved in selecting new tenants for vacant flats, the housing authority have provided resident janitors to improve security, and the landscape design has further reinforced this by enclosing the internal courtyards with walls and creating a hierarchy of spaces within this. The master plan was produced in 1984 and was seen as a flexible document, which would change in the light of both response to the initial phases and to funding and employment opportunities as these arose.

Barrowfield was almost a self-contained enclave as traffic management policies had limited access into the estate to two points, blocking off other entrance roads. There was no clear circulation pattern, a situation compounded by an uncompleted section of dual carriageway and surface car parking, which effectively split the site. Front gardens were derelict and trees destroyed; broken glass littered the streets. Boarded-up windows and graffiti on the walls to the access stairs added to this picture of urban dereliction. Behind the buildings, the back courts were overgrown and neglected, a rank wasteland of litter and rubbish, used as short cuts across the estate and shunned by residents, particularly after dark.

The master plan aimed to overcome these problems by a comprehensive policy of environmental improvement. Back courtyards were made private to the residents adjacent to them by connecting the blocks with brick walls and securing access passages with lockable doors and gates. From this secure base, improvements implemented with the involvement of the particular residents are virtually assured of success. The residents provide their own surveillance to the space, any anti-social behaviour or wilful damage can be connected to an individual or family and the problem dealt with locally. A perception of 'them and us' is replaced by 'one of ours', an identity with something that we, the community, have helped create.

In Phase One of Barrowfield the success of this policy is obvious on the ground. The area has an overall containment, reinforced by the gradually diminishing size of the spaces closer to the houses. The landform has been remodelled to sub-divide the space into three types of area, each one facing a housing block. Crescent-shaped areas of grass provide for informal ball-games. Clothes-drying areas are next to the houses, fenced and paved for further security and identity. Planting is concentrated along the ridges of the central mound, mainly as large shrubs and trees. The species used are hard wearing and fast growing – *Sambucus nigra, Cornus alba, Berberis thunbergii* (Fig.3.9). The space is heavily used, particularly by children. In winter the path across the mound provides an unplanned sledging run.

This scheme also provided a fair level of employment for locals. The management contractor engaged local unemployed men onto his permanent staff. Subcontracts were given to Community Businesses for fencing and painting. A local person was given the permanent job as janitor, funded by the housing authority. (During production of this book the Community Business Company ceased trading. Nonetheless, the Barrowfield Strategy continues to be used as the model for rehabilitating similar housing areas in Central Scotland, at Dundee, Edinburgh, Glasgow and Paisley.)

CONCLUSIONS

In March 1987, to mark the end of the first ten years of the partnership project, the members of the GEAR governing committee signed a declaration of continuing commitment to the area. This is to safeguard and build on the financial, social and economic investments the participants have made in the whole area. In this period £33 million was spent on improving derelict or vacant land, including planting and maintenance. As evidence of their continuing commitment, the SDA will provide £13 million over the next three years. With this public investment it expects to attract some £55 million in private funding for industry, commerce and housing (Fig.3.10).

Landscape architects have been involved at all levels in the planning, implementation and establishment of the GEAR project. They are represented at the strategic level, within the contributing authorities such as the SDA, SSHA and the Regional and District Authorities. As consultants they have prepared planning and landscape studies ranging in scope from the Clyde Corridor through to the Barrowfield Project. They have prepared project designs and supervised their construction and subsequent maintenance. Now landscape designers and managers within the Glasgow District will be responsible for ensuring the continuing development of this large investment in environmental improvement. The GEAR project shows clearly the need for landscape designers to be aware of particular conditions – social, economic and environmental. Linked to this is a requirement to build into the design and enabling process a system to ensure the establishment, maintenance and management of the project. There must be a continuing revenue commitment to safeguard the initial capital cost of all schemes.

The system of establishment and maintenance contracts evolved for GEAR seems a useful model, particularly for environmental improvement projects. In these, the growing conditions for plant material are usually extremely poor, and there is a consequent need to give careful attention to such schemes during the establishment phase.

Also the GEAR Environmental Study has used some of these contracts as test beds to experiment with various management techniques. Their findings have been integrated into their reports, and should prove useful in the long term to the local authority Parks Department. They provide a basis for ensuring the continuing development of these environmental improvements as a long-term asset to the communities who work, live and play there.

3.9   Simple earth mounding, reinforced by bold tree and shrub planting, successfully humanizes a previously bleak and derelict courtyard in the Barrowfield Project.

3.10   (Next page) By upgrading the older flats and reclaiming adjacent derelict sites, the GEAR project has attracted private housing into the area.

4

New town design
The Diplomatic Quarter, Ar-riyadh

INTRODUCTION

This case study is an excellent example of the need to harness applied research to the design process. It also demonstrates the benefit of a strong co-ordinating client authority, which can control, guide and influence all stages of the design process, from briefing through to establishment and maintenance. This close relationship between client, consultant and academics has resulted, for instance, in the successful use of native species for much of the planting.

The decision to move the foreign embassies and diplomatic corps from Jeddah to the capital, Ar-riyadh (Riyadh), was taken in 1985. Ar-riyadh itself was going through a rapid expansion in both population and built development. The 1985 population was estimated at 900,000, an increase of 75 per cent since 1975. It is projected to reach one million in 1995 and stabilize thereafter. This urban expansion follows the plans of the Ar-riyadh Development Authority (ADA).

The Diplomatic Quarter is situated to the west of the city on the edge of Wadi Hanifah. Ar-riyadh lies in the climatically arid Central Region of Saudi Arabia, at an elevation of 590m (1920ft) The summers are hot and dry, with temperatures sometimes in excess of 45°C. Winters are relatively cooler, with a mean minimum temperature of 17.2°C. The wind is persistent: hot and dry from the south-west in summer, cooler and infrequently rain-bearing from the north-west in winter. The mean precipitation is 89mm (3½in.), falling in winter and spring as infrequent thunderstorms and cloudbursts. The relative humidity, however, is only 43 per cent. Thus if protection can be given from the excessive effects of wind and solar radiation, the outdoor climate for at least half the year is relatively pleasant. This is seen from the present seasonal and temporal pattern of open-space use in Ar-riyadh and the surrounding desert and date farms. During the hotter summer months, the traditional family picnics take place in the evenings, usually in the shade of the date palms. During the cooler months, secluded desert depressions are also used during weekend evenings.

An understanding of these traditional forms of recreation and their response to various factors such as culture, topography, climate and vegetation were an integral part of the planning and design brief for the new Diplomatic Quarter. This was not to be a compound solely for foreign embassies and their staffs. Rather it was planned from the beginning as a complete new sector, containing a spine-like central commercial core, five residential neighbourhoods with appropriate social facilities and a carefully organized circulation system for both vehicles and pedestrians. Diplomats and local Saudis were to live next to each other. Open space was seen as an essential part of the plan and had to be integrated with the built development.

In the commercial spine and within the housing areas the open spaces are intensively planted and managed. Over half the area of open space, however, is treated in an extensive, low-key manner, to integrate the planting with the adjacent Wadi Hanifa, and the peripheral desert environment. This also makes the best use of the limited water budget, by restricting irrigation to those areas most intensively used by the population. These decisions were arrived at after studies and experiments carried out by both landscape consultants and a technical committee of academics and government agents to suggest, test and monitor techniques for designing with, and establishing, native plant stock.

This extensive approach to planting employs techniques that have been used in Europe, but mainly in land reclamation or for individual construction projects in the countryside. The Diplomatic Quarter is a unique example of their application on such a scale and for an urban development. It has lessons that are applicable not only to similar climatic regions, but the principles of seed collection and propagation also have wider relevance to other arid regions.

THE PLANNING AND DESIGN PROCESS

The planning, design and construction of the Diplomatic Quarter is co-ordinated by a supervising group of professional officers in the Ar-riyadh Development Authority (ADA) under the leadership of the Right Honourable Mohammed Al-Shaikh. The master plan was prepared by a team of planning consultants in 1978[1] and this document has been broadly followed by detailed development designs. In 1981 landscape consultants were appointed for the design and implementation phases of the so-called 'Intensive' and 'Extensive' landscaping. Intensive landscaping includes 23 public parks, street planting, open spaces in the commercial spine and within the residential neighbourhoods, and private areas associated with individual developments such as the International School and Diplomatic Club.

The design of the extensive landscaping area aims to link the new development to the adjacent wadi both visually and environmentally while providing facilities for outdoor activities, which are not found in the designated public parks. It included a plan to provide a pedestrian network to connect the wadi with the neighbourhood housing and to contain sitting-, play- and picnic-areas, sports facilities and examples of semi-natural habitats. These habitats were to include flat and dune arid areas and wet oasis-like areas so as to introduce a wider range of native plant species. In both intensive and extensive areas, great care was taken to respect the traditional social and cultural values of the local people, especially with respect to family privacy.

ORGANIZATION

Since 1984 the authority with responsibility for the establishment of the Diplomatic Quarter has been the ADA. This superseded the Bureau for the Diplomatic Quarter, which had been established in 1976 to supervise and facilitate the physical movement of the Ministry of Foreign Affairs and the Embassies from Jeddah. The ADA has similar powers to those of a British Urban Development Authority or a New Town Authority. All municipal powers are vested in this small organization of about 80 persons. Once the Quarter is fully developed and established it is expected that the Municipality of Ar-riyadh will take over most of the day-to-day civic responsibilities.

Under their Chief Executive or President, Dr Mohammed Al-Shaikh, the ADA is divided into two main sections: project planning and research; and contracts, operations and maintenance. Each section is headed by a Director General. There are further subdivisions within each section. Those that bear most closely on the landscape policy are the projects for planning; the architecture and landscape groups; and the contracts and maintenance section.

The projects planning and architecture teams control all aspects of development in the Diplomatic Quarter, either directly as client, or through their development control authority when dealing with embassies or private developments. All the design work is contracted out to consultants. The ADA is closely involved during the design stage to ensure that its standards are met. This is achieved by a series of design reviews, when the consultants' proposals are evaluated against the Project Brief. Also the qualifications of all consultants – and, at contract stage, all contractors – and their staff are checked to ensure that they are competent to carry out the work to a good standard.

Once a contract is let, the ADA responsibility moves to the contracts section, who provide a site team to check and monitor all work, to ensure that drawings and construction meet the required specification. Then on completion, all public areas are maintained by the maintenance section, who check stakes and irrigation systems, carry out any feeding, thinning or pruning of plants, control weeds and pests and collect litter. This section also incorporates the Diplomatic Quarter plant nursery, which was established to improve the quality and range of plant material. Stock is either propagated in the nursery, or bought locally and grown on. Contractors working in the Diplomatic Quarter are encouraged to use plants from the nursery where possible. If plants from another source are used, then these must be of the same quality as from the nursery – a readily verifiable standard.

TIME-SCALE AND BRIEF

Until 1957 Ar-riyadh was a closed city to foreigners. It still retained much of the character of a small densely-developed desert town, walled for defence against intruders and the elements. At this date the Government Ministries, with the exception of Foreign Affairs, were moved to Ar-riyadh.

Foreign Affairs remained in Jeddah, where the foreign embassies and trade delegations had become established; partly as a result of the traditional trading role of Jeddah, and partly to cope with the influx of pilgrims for the annual Hadj at Makkah.

In 1975 the Government decided to bring the Foreign Affairs Ministry to Ar-riyadh, together with the foreign embassies. At that time some 81 Ambassadors were accredited to the Kingdom. The original strategy was that the Diplomatic Corps would have moved to Ar-riyadh by 1985 and be established in the new Diplomatic Quarter by 1987. By

April 1987 some 20 embassies were open, a further 17 under construction and over 30 at the building design stage. Given the original ambitious timetable, this progress is good. The Diplomatic Quarter already has an appearance of being well established, largely as a result of the forward thinking of the designers in establishing early on both the structure planting in the central spine area and the circulation systems as major elements from the master plan.

The master plan, prepared by German consultants, was begun in May 1977 and completed in late 1978. In 1981 additional land to the south was added to the site and incorporated into the master plan. The brief was not only to rehouse the embassies and their staff but also to create the equivalent of a new city neighbourhood, with a final population of some 25,000 persons. Of this final population 50 per cent was to be native Saudis, as the Government wished to avoid establishing a closed community solely composed of the diplomatic corps. It was important to see the new development as an integral part of the planned growth of Al-riyadh.

MASTER PLAN (Fig. 4.1).

Managing Consultants, appointed in May 1977, were Speerplan of Frankfurt, in partnership with Heinle Wischer of Stuttgart and Rhein-Ruhr Ingenieur-Gesellschaft of Dortmund. Bodeker Boyer Wagenfeld & Partners (BBW) of Dusseldorf acted as landscape consultants to the master plan team. In essence the plan consists of a linear central spine of commercial facilities sandwiched between the embassy compounds. Attached to these are five residential areas, each containing local facilities such as shops, mosques and schools. Specialized functions such as the Sports Centre, the Diplomatic Club and the International School take advantage of existing natural features in central locations. The main interest in terms of landscape design, however, is the manner in which this simple concept has been adjusted in response to both the general and specific environmental characteristics of the site and the local social and cultural patterns.

The site, including the southern extension added in 1981, extends to over 800 ha (2000 acres) in area. It lies some 8km (5 miles) to the north-west of the centre of Riyadh. Some 3km (2 miles) in length, it was bounded on the east and south by proposed motorways, on the west by Wadi Hanifah and on the north by a tributary wadi. Basically the site is a limestone plateau, overlain by a thin overburden of the weathered bedrock in the form of silts and gravels. From a high point of 665m (2180ft) in the south-west, the plateau slopes gently to the northwest, some 30m (98ft) lower.

There is undulating land in this south-east corner, with low hillocks some 40m (130ft) above the general level. Contrasting with this typically desert landscape is the green ravine of the Wadi Hanifah and its three tributaries, which form the western and northern site boundaries. This area of deep alluvial soil lies some 30m (98ft) below the plateau. It is mainly under date palm cultivation and contains an oasis settlement, Arqah. Although not part of the Diplomatic Quarter site, the Wadi Hanifah is a major influence in terms of microclimate, drainage and scenic quality.

Speerplan identified three zones, each with a distinct landscape character: the gently-sloping central zone; the undulating south-east corner of the site; and the wadi edge. Each zone suggested different types and intensity of development, ranging from minimal constraints for development on the plateau to maximum constraints on the wadi edge. The hilly area restricted major buildings to the shallower slopes. This simple description of the three landscape zones conceals the manner in which they actually interact and how the wadis penetrate the plateau and the hillocks ripple across the eastern edge. This gives rise to a subtle change in range and aspect of view, which the consultants cleverly utilized to integrate the existing environment into the new development.

Four other environmental factors influenced the final form of the master plan: the requirements for shade to circulation routes and external areas; the need for

4.1   **The master plan for the Diplomatic Quarter.**
(*Speerplan.*)

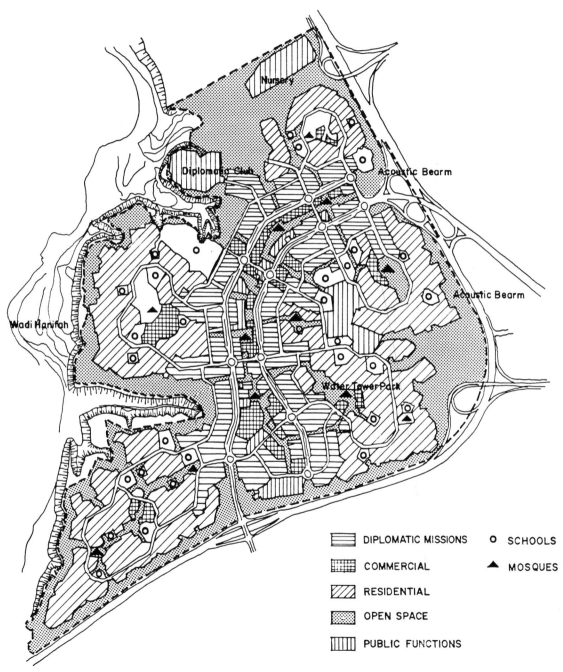

DIPLOMATIC MISSIONS   ○ SCHOOLS

COMMERCIAL   ▲ MOSQUES

RESIDENTIAL

OPEN SPACE

PUBLIC FUNCTIONS

controlled air flow through the major open spaces; the need to minimize the amount of irrigation water; and the need to create sound barriers.

These last three points also influenced the surface water drainage pattern. Shade and ventilation considerations also determined the suggested built form – dense and low buildings with major roads at right angles to the prevailing winds to prevent long, wide channels accelerating the speed of dust-laden wind from the desert. Open spaces were to be linear in form, and connecting with the wadi. Planting would reduce the air temperatures, and also filter out dust.

An irrigation master plan was also prepared, using two lines, one potable water, the other treated sewage effluent. The pipes for these are carried in a general services' trench, which also contained electricity, telephones and sewage. The trenches were installed throughout the Diplomatic Quarter site in the first phase of infrastructure development. This meant that overall structural planting could be established in advance of built development, initially using only potable water for irrigation.

In form the planting and open-space structure develops two contrasting patterns, the linear spine of the central facilities and major roads, and the radial extensions of the wadis penetrating through the spine and converging at the Sports Centre (Fig. 4.2). In addition the acoustic berm contains the development on the east and south, reinforcing the focus of open-space structure towards the Wadi Hanifah. In design and management terms the planting concept was broadly divided into two systems, intensive

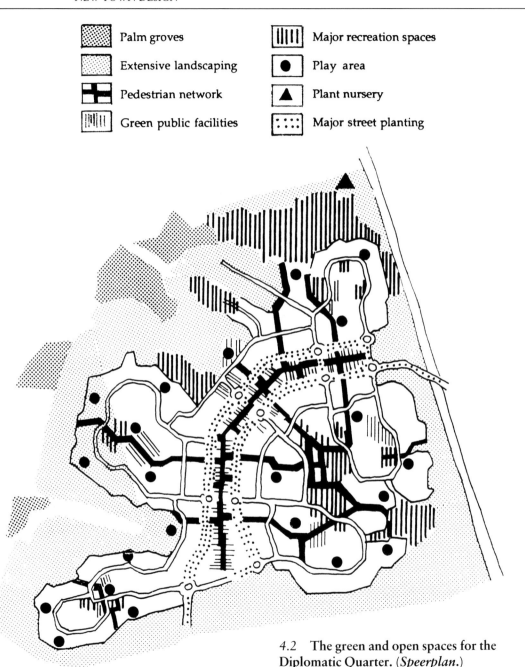

Palm groves

Extensive landscaping

Pedestrian network

Green public facilities

Major recreation spaces

Play area

Plant nursery

Major street planting

4.2   The green and open spaces for the Diplomatic Quarter. (*Speerplan.*)

and extensive, as mentioned above. These were a response to the perceived influences of existing vegetation and soil, the estimated water budget for potential irrigation, recreational demands and the desire to blend the new Diplomatic Quarter sensitively into the surrounding landscape. As the terms imply, the intensive areas rely on irrigated nursery stock, whilst extensive plant material is in the main native and unirrigated once established. The surface drainage, however, is designed to feed these areas, so that natural rainfall is used in the most beneficial manner to sustain vegetation.

The design of the intensive areas is greatly varied, as they include the highly-urban commercial spine of the central facilities; the streets and pedestrian circulation routes; the parks and play areas; the private development areas such as the embassies and their residencies; and housing areas. The central core contains an interior pedestrian route, shaded by the buildings or pergolas (Fig. 4.3). Open squares provide shaded seating complemented by water features and formal planting beds. The radial pedestrian routes cross the core at these points and continue into the embassy areas. Here they are shaded

4.3   **The shade afforded by a reinforced concrete pergola on a pedestrian circulation route.**

by trees and pergolas and sitting and play areas occur along them. As they penetrate the housing areas, they link up to the schools and to neighbourhood centres, mosques and formal parks before merging back into the natural, extensive areas along the wadi or the acoustic berm. This hierarchical system suggested by the progression from the central spine outwards to the neighbourhoods is reinforced by the scale and formal pattern of tree planting used for the vehicular and pedestrian routes. Four to five rows of date palms (*Phoenix dactylifera*) were specified for the main routes and one to two rows for the collector roads. Medium crowned trees such as *Delonix regia*, *Prosopis chilensis* or *Parkinsonia aculeata* were used on the smaller access roads to give identity to separate areas.

Within the intensive zone the housing areas and embassy and residency compounds form privately landscaped areas. A series of planting codes have been developed, related to the available irrigation water, to which private developments must adhere. Thus each embassy or residency must provide one tree for each square 100m (1070ft); each private house plot is required to have one tree to the front of the dwelling, one to the rear and one in the patio.

The extensive landscaping, which occupies some 40 per cent of the site, is not dealt with at great length in the master plan but as a later part of this chapter will discuss, this part evolved into the most innovative aspect of the open space design in the Diplomatic Quarter. The master plan itself, however, merely defined both the need to minimize the amount of irrigation required and the important role vegetation plays in combating strong winds and filtering sand and dust.

Ten years on (April 1987) from the submission of the master plan, there is sufficient development completed or in progress to evaluate its successes and failures. One important decision that has helped ensure a feeling of maturity was to install the entire infrastructure of roads and servicing as phase one. This has allowed the structure planting to become established in advance of building contracts and has been particularly important in the designated housing areas.

Due, however, to changing attitudes, for security reasons, towards an open Diplomatic Quarter integrated with native Saudis, governmental permission to develop the five housing areas has been withheld. This has left areas of undeveloped wasteland between the tree-lined access roads and pedestrian walkways. In contrast to British new and expanding town developments, where the early residents are given homes but no educational, social or health facilities until a certain level of population is reached, here things are reversed. All the supporting facilities such as schools, clinics and mosques are complete but there are few homes. However, this will surely change. Two other developments occurred subsequent to the master plan submission: a change to the neighbourhood access roads, and the substitution of a public park (for the residents of Ar-riyadh) for the golf course proposed for the northern wadi. The access roads to the housing areas were planned to terminate as simple turning circles. At the suggestion of a Saudi architect, Farhad Tashkandi, however, these were re-designed as cul-de-sacs with combined pedestrian and vehicular use and phased into the contract drawings as work progressed. This helps create local meeting points, and they have been designed with this in mind, incorporating simple play equipment, seating and shade planting.

The golf course was omitted for two reasons, one being that the site of the old Ar-riyadh airport is to be developed as a large recreational area including a golf course. It was also felt important that the Diplomatic Quarter provide a public facility for the residents of Ar-riyadh to encourage them to consider the new quarter as truly a part of the city. Thus the northern wadi is now being developed as a public park but with an educational bias. It will have a Botanical Garden to display plants and landforms from seven deserts of the world (Fig.4.4).

The majority of the elements of the master plan have been carried through, are being implemented or are under consideration for future contracts. Already the impact of the open space structure is obvious, particularly the acoustic berm and the planting along roads and pedestrian routes. These, together with the green finger of Wadi Hanifah, give the Diplomatic Quarter a strong sense of identity, one that both combines new elements with old and shows an intelligent response to existing landscape character. As the resident population grows, it will find not only all the built facilities associated with urban life but also appropriate recreational facilities, parks and family picnic areas. Indeed some of the parks are already so well used by families from Ar-riyadh at weekends that control on their use is being considered by the ADA.

4.4 **The public park sites in the northern wadi, below the Diplomatic Club. Surface water run-off collected in the gully provides a potential seasonal wetland habitat.**

EXTENSIVE LANDSCAPE

The design contract for the so-called extensive planting was given to the German consultants, BBW of Dusseldorf in October 1981. This included the 100m (327ft) deep strip along the entire edge of Wadi Hanifah, the three tributary wadis and the acoustic berm alongside the motorways on the eastern and southern boundaries. The brief stated that planting in this zone was to be native in character, using both indigenous and adapted species.

The master plan considered the extensive zone as acting as a transition between the developed urban areas of the site and the natural edge of Wadi Hanifah and the desert. The berm, acting as a noise barrier, utilized excavated materials from the basements and foundations of the buildings – some excavations extended to 17m (55½ft). The surface-water drainage channels collect runoff from all buildings and paved areas and are designed to appear and act as small wadis. This means that the natural character of land-form, surface materials and planting penetrates into the heart of the built development, avoiding an obvious transition. These new wadis, together with the existing tributary wadis, can sustain a richer, more diverse range of plants than the more arid plateau edge and berm areas (Fig.4.5). Soil conditions, exposure and aspect all change rapidly throughout the site depending on subtle variations in land-form, orientation and location. The challenge for the designers was to respond to these in a way that developed these micro-site conditions, whilst at the same time ensuring that the special recreational needs of the residents were met, and that maintenance factors, particularly irrigation, were carefully considered.

The brief, evolved in discussions between the ADA and the landscape consultants, suggested the need for a pedestrian network to connect the main view-points and cultural features – such as the old kilns and watch-towers – and to link with the housing areas

4.5 Local stone and native plants establish the natural character of the acoustic berm. The landform is built up from material excavated during building construction within the Diplomatic Quarter.

and the Wadi Hanifah. The main route would also provide a variety of facilities such as parks and sports facilities (the Speerplan master plan had proposed about 20 local parks in the extensive zone), sitting and play areas, picnic alcoves including parking, with appropriate servicing and as wide a range as possible of Saudi Central Region habitats. This habitat creation was to have an educational as well as recreational role, stimulating an interest in and consequent respect for the natural environment in both diplomats and native Saudis.

The extensive design project was extremely complex and very innovative within the Kingdom. It was the first time that planting of native species had been carried out on such a large scale. Client, consultant and contractor were largely learning as the contract proceeded, and there were some failures with planting. However, it is greatly to the credit of all concerned that, through discussions with local experts and carefully monitored experiments, sensible and largely-successful planting methods have evolved (Fig. 4.6).

To complement the planting design, the land-form and construction materials were also kept as natural as possible. The berm

4.6   **The planting in this area was established using native seeds, and largely without irrigation. (M. Salama.)**

resembles a sand dune in form, sinuously wrapping around the eastern and southern site boundaries, pierced only by the main access road from Ar-riyadh. This enters below the highest point of the berm, about 37m (120ft) above normal ground level, which reinforces the visitor's sense of arrival. Indeed the approach by road from Ar-riyadh is one of opening and closing views. Travelling from the main roundabout on the freeway the focus is the walled silhouette of the Diplomatic Club, then the berm shuts out all views of the site, offering instead an undulating slope with pockets of acacia, and alongside the road a small wadi-like drainage channel. This contains a lusher vegetation, including many annuals. A canyon-like opening sweeps one through the berm and onto the main boulevard, signalled by a roundabout crowned with flagpoles (Fig. 4.7). This is an important junction between the extensive and intensive zones, forming a contrasting juxtaposition of dense irrigated planting with more sparse native species.

A path follows the ridge of the berm and culminates in a viewing platform on the highest point. The path is surfaced with flat, undressed stone slabs and is depressed into

4.7   The roundabout at the entrance to the Diplomatic Quarter, seen from the acoustic berm. The empty spaces are planned housing areas.

the land-form, between retaining walls of similar stone. Planting occurs in natural-looking depressions, mainly dominated by *Acacia arabica, Caparis spinosa* and *Calotropis procera*. Bays for sitting are often next to these planted areas to take advantage of shade. There are panoramic views from this ridge walk, over Ar-riyadh to the east, and the Diplomatic Quarter to the west. From here the physical containment of the Quarter by the berm and Wadi Hanifah is very apparent, as is the open-space structure, despite the empty spaces designated for residential development.

Inside the berm, the landscape character changes subtly. Here a wet habitat has been created by leading surface runoff into an open, wadi-like drainage system (see Fig.4.4). This leads back into the existing natural wadi system and extends a natural habitat into future housing areas. In the north-east some old brickmaking kilns have been retained as a centre piece to a sitting area.

On the edge of Wadi Hanifah, this blending of intensive use with extensive landscape has also been followed, probably most successfully on the southern tributary wadi (Fig.4.8). Here a deliberate attempt has been

4.8 **Path above Wadi Hanifah, overlooking the wadi palm groves. Stone walls and paving simulate the natural sandstone strata. The planting is native and unirrigated.**

made to reinforce existing local topography to create a range of desert habitats, ranging from a new sand dune to an oasis. An informal sports area, serviced sitting areas and picnic alcoves are also provided. All these elements are linked to the pedestrian routes, and all plant material is native. This gives an overall continuity to the area and also eliminates the need for any irrigation. In this, one of the latest sections to be completed, the natural approach to design has been most successfully achieved. The spaces created for the diverse functions such as games, family socializing and picnicking appear wholly natural as if the landscape designer has been fortunate enough to find already existing spaces that fitted the functional requirements. In fact large areas have been manipulated, particularly the sand dune and the sports area, which says much for the design ability of all those involved (see Fig. 4.6).

In some of the park areas this blend between new function and natural form has not been so successfully achieved, with obviously manufactured and formal elements crowding and dominating the natural elements to the detriment of both. This is most apparent at the central wadi, where pierced metal shelters and coursed, dressed-stone walls in the formal park dominate the head of the rocky wadi and overpower the subtleties of this apparently natural area (Fig. 4.9). This seems to be mainly a result of an unsuccessful juxtaposition of contrasting forms and elements. A similar park in another housing area relates extremely well to the surrounding mosque, kindergarten and embassies.

4.9 **In this formal park, the pierced metal roof of a pavilion creates a pattern of light and shadow in sharp contrast to the unshaded exterior.**

INTENSIVE DESIGN

Only two elements from this area will be considered in detail: the central area, including the boulevard planting and the pedestrian spines, and two public parks.

The landscape design for the central area was carried out by Robert Carter of Los Angeles, in association with a local Ar-riyadh firm, Omrania, beginning in April 1983. The contract contained three main sections comprising the pedestrian circulation within the central facilities; the planting and roundabout design for the main arterial roads or so-called boulevards; and the main pedestrian network. This involved close co-operation with the road engineers and with the urban designer and architect responsible for the central spine, Ali Shuaibi.

The central spine is about half completed. It contains a basement area for car parking and servicing which means that the pedestrian spine is effectively a roof deck, and all planting is into artificial conditions, requiring imported soil and permanent irrigation (Fig.4.10). The external spaces are also directly dictated by the shape, scale and massing of the buildings that in effect form the floor, edge and often the roof.

In this case the architect has used traditional Najd (central) region architectural forms and materials, to evoke a walled, inward-looking complex, uniform in height, colour and texture. The only contrast comes from the square minarets of the Friday Mosque, which acts as a landmark throughout the Diplomatic Quarter. The external spaces are a series of

4.10   Recent planting in the central commercial spine. Trees on the edge of the courtyard will give shade to the seats. (M. Salama.)

courtyards, varying in size and connected by covered passages through the buildings. These connections are reminiscent of souks, as they open onto shops and offices at street level and are overlooked by two storeys of flats and offices reached by galleries. Horizontal textile canopies at first-floor level provide shade and privacy for these upper levels, whilst geometrically-pierced openings in the ceiling combine the advantages of air movements with further shade and attractive patterning.

The landscape designer has set out to complement the geometry of the buildings in the treatment of the squares and courtyards. Planting is on a regular grid, responding to the structural requirements imposed by the car deck below. Tree planting is designed to create both shade and contrast with the largely flat, unmodelled building façades. Shrubs, ground cover plants and climbers provide another contrast in texture and colour to the uniform brown of the buildings. At present the planting is immature, and final judgement should be reserved. It does seem, however, rather regimented and unimaginative, and not sufficiently bold in mass or in character to complement, let alone create a balance with, the dominant architecture. In contrast, the planting along the boulevards or arterial roads is bold, forceful and in scale with the speed of vehicular traffic.

Too often in roadside planting, designers achieve a rhythm or pattern to their planting that is more akin to the speed of pedestrian travel. When viewed from a moving car this becomes busy and confusing as too many varieties of plants are used for the human eye to establish a pattern at such speed.

Here, however, the plant species are sensibly restricted, with single species planted in sufficiently large groups to register as a distinct pattern. Large drifts of *Carpobrotus edululus, Carissa grandiflora 'Green carpet', Gazania leucoleana, Ipomoea pes-caprae* and *Rosmarinus officinalae 'Prostratus'* underplant the regular avenue planting of *Phoenix dactylifera*. At roundabouts, *Acacia sp, Agave Americana, Aloe vera, Atriplex sp, Bouganvillea sp., Dodonea viscosa* and *Thevetia nerifolia* are also used. In addition to planting, several roundabouts also incorporate fountains and sculpture or, in the case of that at the main entrance to the quarter, a forest of flagpoles. Local limestone gravel is used as a mulch under all planting, to minimize water loss and to provide a more natural setting for the planting (Fig. 4.11).

The aim of the street planting has been to achieve a high-quality entrance and approach to the central area and the embassies. Shading the road to prevent glare and solar gain was important, as was shade for the adjacent footpaths. These aims have largely been achieved, and orientation for visitors is helped by the varied design of the roundabouts, though some of these are not entirely successful. Shade was an even more important consideration in the design of the separate pedestrian network. The master plan concept was that paths would radiate out from the Sports Centre, like spokes of a wheel, piercing the central spine to merge with the three tributary wadis (see Fig. 4.2). They were

intended to connect the neighbourhood educational facilities and mosques, and provide incidental sitting and play areas at points along the network. Shading is provided by adjacent buildings, a specially designed pergola and trees. In the proposed residential areas the buildings are not yet constructed, so there the shading comes from only the pergolas and the trees. Indeed, in these locations the spine seems rather incongruous, a finger of green passing through a wasteland. However, once the housing is developed, the residents will surely appreciate these mature routes for the shade and protection they offer

(see Fig.4.3). In detail, the pre-cast concrete pergolas are rather massive structures, and tend to dominate both the spaces they control and the climbers that are attempting to swathe them. Something more delicate and lighter in appearance would have been less visually obtrusive. The incidental spaces are generally carefully designed to provide variety of scale and of facilities provided. The use of planting here is also intelligent, with an interesting mix of species chosen for their contrast in form and texture. Most are adapted species, appropriate in an area that will be irrigated.

The second landscape element to be considered is neighbourhood park design. Two contrasting parks, one from Housing Area 2 and the other the Water Tower Garden, located at the base of the two water towers, will be discussed. Both were designed by the German consultants, BBW, but are completely different in design concept and choice of materials. One is extremely formal in layout and highly finished in terms of materials and construction, the other aims for a largely natural appearance with a free-form plan and uses undressed stone and gravel as materials.

The formal park is laid out around the neighbourhood mosque and is bounded on the east by a local distributor road. It consists of four main elements: a formal grove of trees on the north, connecting the mosque to the yet unbuilt local shopping area; a children's play area; a simple grassed area; and a formal enclosed garden, distinctly Moorish in design (Fig. 4.12). Each of these areas meets a different need in the social and recreational patterns of local Saudis.

The area of trees – *Eucalyptus cameldulensis* – aims for a very formal, almost architectural, relationship with the

4.11 *(Left)* **The planting along the main road axis uses native and adapted species. A gravel mulch restricts weed growth and limits evaporation from the soil.**

4.12 *(Right)* **Moorish design concepts have strongly influenced this formal park layout.**

mosque. Unlike the other areas it is unwalled and will be open to the adjacent shopping area. It can act as a casual meeting place, around prayer times and on shopping trips. The adjacent children's play area reflects this mixed function, as fathers can supervise their children here without disturbing the privacy of family groups in the formal and grassed areas. These last two areas are to cater for family groups, either in defined pavilion-like shelters in the formal garden by day or on the grass during the cooler evenings. Each is enclosed by dressed stone walls over 2m (6½ft) in height and pierced at regular

intervals by metal grilles. Entry is controlled by metal gates.

The formal area is surrounded by an intricate timber pergola, carried from the external wall. Pavilions at regular intervals provide discrete and cool sitting areas for family groups to gather, off the circulation route. Each element focuses on the garden. The central feature of this is a shallow cruciform water channel with a series of water jets in a semi-circular pattern (Fig. 4.12). This is reminiscent of gardens in the Generalife in Granada and the Alcazar in Cordoba. The materials are restricted to

4.13 **The natural appearance of the Water Tower park is created from rocks, gravel and native plants.**

dressed stone walls and paving, with gravel in the main courtyard, and patterned timber screens and pergolas. These simple elements are, however, considerably enriched by the changing patterns of sunlight cast by the screens and pergolas onto both horizontal and vertical surfaces.

In contrast to this geometric design, which uses historic Islamic precedents as models, the Water Tower Garden attempts to create a natural appearance of rocky forms and native or adapted plants. It is located at the highest point on the plateau, around the base of the two elegant water towers. These towers, although over 70m (230ft) high, do not overpower the space, due partly to their simple and elegant form, but mainly because the park is cleverly broken down into a series of small spaces each with its own focus of interest. Although a central space has been designed here, the eye is constantly led to the smaller peripheral niches created by craggy upright rocks, flat irregular paving stones, gravel and profuse ground-cover planting mainly of *Iomea sp* and *Gazania sp*. (Fig. 4.13). Although the park is walled, being high up the views across the Diplomatic Quarter and to Ar-riyadh are not obstructed, and from most areas the park seems to flow into the surrounding desert landscape.

Large boulders are used to create enclosure and shade and act as impromptu seats. Trees which can tolerate arid conditions, such as *Acacia arabia* and *Parkinsonia aculeata*, reinforce the shade and character. Flat, irregular paving stones define areas and paths and contain the gravel mulch that covers the majority of the surface. Over this sprawls the richly-coloured ground cover. Floodlighting ensures that these desert-like areas are usable during the evening, when most family parties come to the open spaces.

SPECIAL RECREATION AREAS –
THE DIPLOMATIC CLUB

Two specialized recreational facilities have been provided in the Diplomatic Quarter: a Sports Centre and a Diplomatic Club. The Sports Centre, as described in the master plan, is to act as the hub of the spokes of the green fingers of the pedestrian network, radiating outwards to join the existing green valley of the Wadi Hanifah. The Diplomatic Club is to act as a social and recreational area for the diplomatic community, combining some of the functions of a first-class hotel and a country club. It has hotel accommodation for visitors, dining areas, conference suites, swimming pools and outdoor tennis courts. The site is on the promontory between the northern and central tributary wadis, overlooking the palm-filled Wadi Hanifah. This is one of the most prominent locations in the Diplomatic Quarter as any building here is seen from the freeway approaches to the Quarter and is also constantly visible from the wadi edge. It contains two landscape zones, the plateau and the wadi edge and straddles the extensive and intensive design areas. It is obvious that any development on this site must be handled extremely sensitively.

As a result of a limited international competition, the ADA asked the consultants responsible for two entries – Frei Otto of Stuttgart and Omrania of Riyadh – to prepare a joint proposal. The brilliant solution owes little to either of the original designs. Rather it is a reappraisal of the means by which built form can be used – in both technically traditional and innovative ways – to overcome difficult environmental factors and create useful and attractive internal and external spaces.

The building has two main elements, a sinuous, stone-clad hollow wall that encloses an open courtyard and a series of tensile tents that hang from both interior and exterior surfaces of the wall. The wall is the protector, offering defence against the desert wind and solar gain from the desert sun. Outside, the desert environment reigns right up to the foot of the wall. Inside the protective wall – containing up to three storeys of rooms – is an oasis-like sheltered environment, with lush, irrigated planting, creating a cool external space where diplomats and their guests can relax under the palm trees or by the open-air pool. The tents – or 'Desert Roses' as Frei Otto calls them – offer a protected view into either desert or oasis environments. This gives intriguing contrasts both architecturally between the solidity of the wall and the lightness of the tent and between the sophisticated interiors of the 'Roses' and the natural desert landscape outside.

Seen from a distance the Diplomatic Club is an exciting building, which sits simply on the land form. It complements the finger-like promontory that pushes the plateau into Wadi Hanifah. The curvilinear form lightens what might otherwise be a heavy building mass, and the restricted materials do not compete with the colour and texture of the landscape (Fig. 4.14). Closer to, one appreciates the deliberate attempt to retain the desert, or extensive, landscape as an external setting for the building. This is largely achieved by depressing the outdoor

4.14 The Diplomatic Club above Wadi Hanifah presents a largely solid exterior wall to the desert landscape.

games areas and building natural-looking rock walls to the pedestrian path along the top of the wadi. Thus the eye is carried over these formal areas by a foreground of natural materials and native plants. Floodlighting is on retractable posts, so these vertical elements are largely eliminated during daylight. Obviously from within these games areas the illusion of a direct connection with the desert is somewhat lost.

A huge arch leads through the wall and into the enclosed courtyard. Here the contrast is at once marked. Under a canopy of date palms, grass, shrubs and ground covers grow in profusion. Construction materials are still, however, restricted to natural materials or colours, such as stone, gravel and sand-coloured *in situ* concrete. Floodlighting is part of the design concept, in order to display the plants by night when most use will be made of this area. On the northern edge of the courtyard, the wall steps up to its maximum height in a series of planted tiers. A Desert Rose penetrates the wall in the west, to show a contrasting landscape to people inside the building – desert one side, oasis on the other. In the centre sits an open-sided pavilion, roofed with hand-painted glass tiles (Fig. 4.15).

4.15 Inside the protective walls of the Diplomatic Club the landscape designer has created a lush oasis-like environment.

A spiralling ramp climbs from the courtyard up to the top of the wall, as it rises enclosing the swimming-pool area. This contains a children's pool in addition to a circular area for adults. The two are joined by a water slide. Planting species change here to reflect the waterside character. Unfortunately the pools are clad in bright-blue mosaics, which strike an unnatural chord in an otherwise muted colour scheme. A more natural colour – such as buff – would have seemed less attractive to bathers however. Otherwise this is an extremely fine project that illustrates well the concept of two levels of landscape design: extensive and intensive. Here the intensive has been strictly limited to the area that will be most used by Club members in order to make best possible use of the restricted amount of irrigation water. At the same time the surrounding extensive landscape and the existing features such as Wadi Hanifah have been deliberately incorporated both to settle the building into the environment and to give people inside it a sense of contact with the wider, natural landscape.

CONCLUSION

This concluding section aims to emphasize those factors in the design, implementation and maintenance process of this project that have ensured its success, and to discuss any shortfalls or problems which have arisen.

The management of the entire project shows the importance of a close dialogue between client and consultant. The ADA officials were all relatively inexperienced when the project began. The master plan was therefore regarded largely as an educational tool for them. The consultants adopted very much a system of step-by-step explanation of their thought process in arriving at the final form of the master plan and had been actively involved in discussing and testing alternative models during the design stage.

This opportunity to work closely with consultants, and to change parameters when necessary, also occurred during the contracts for the extensive landscaping. Planting of native species on such a scale had not previously been undertaken in the Kingdom, so for all concerned – client, consultant and contractor – it was again a learning exercise. Initially mistakes were made and heavy plant losses occurred.

However, by involving local academics and encouraging experimentation both in seed and plant collection and in planting techniques, successful methods were developed. Seed is now collected from the wild, spread on imported sandy soil (not, as originally, rich wadi soil) and allowed to await germination following natural rainfall. Nursery-grown stock has largely been eliminated from extensive area contracts as such plant material changes its habit and water requirements and has difficulty in readapting to an unirrigated regime.

The plant nursery, which was another recommendation in the master plan, has proved extremely beneficial through supplying good quality plant material to developments within the intensive landscape areas. Previously most plants used in Ar-riyadh were imported and were both expensive and often unable to adapt successfully to their new environment. Using a local source also eliminates the possibility of importing pests or viruses. Now that 97 per cent of the public and structure planting in the Diplomatic Quarter has been completed, the nursery is required to provide only replacement plants. Contractors for embassy or private developments within the Quarter are encouraged to use plants from this source. There is now a feeling that the nursery has fulfilled its role, and consideration is being given to putting it into private hands. A measure of its success is that although it was established solely for the needs of the Diplomatic Quarter by expanding its services it now influences the quality of plant material throughout the Ar-riyadh area.

Maintenance is an important element in the process of landscape design, the factor that ensures that the small plants inserted during the contract are successfully established, continue to grow and fully contribute to the spatial and environmental concepts perceived at the initial design stage. This entails a continuing and long-term commitment to ensure that losses are replaced, stakes are checked, weeds and pests controlled, irrigation monitored and pruning and feeding correctly carried out. Since 1987 the ADA has had a special maintenance section carrying out these duties. Beginning with one water truck and eight men, their numbers had grown to 82 in April 1987. Personnel is expected to grow further as new areas are taken over from contractors.

The standard of planting and maintenance in public areas in the Diplomatic Quarter is probably the highest in the Kingdom of Saudi Arabia. As with new town corporations in the United Kingdom, these management responsibilities will eventually be handed over to the local municipality – Ar-riyadh. There is an obvious danger that the present high standards will no longer be met and that the present quality environment will decline, through either neglect or change in maintenance techniques. It is important that the Municipality understands the level of maintenance required in order to train skilled personnel and ensure an appropriate level of revenue budget. Again, this is a problem common in Britain where professionals at both Milton Keynes and Warrington new towns fear that their landscape management policies will not be adequately followed after handover to local authorities and that the planting quality will rapidly deteriorate.

Another problem that affects the public open spaces, particularly the intensive parks, is overuse and abuse by the public. Over 5000 cars were counted on one weekend in the Diplomatic Quarter gardens. This shows the popularity of the parks, but unfortunately, the pressure of numbers has led to damage to plants and irrigation systems. There have also been complaints from the diplomatic community about the influx of people from outside the Quarter. The main problem is one of lack of similar high quality recreational areas close to Ar-riyadh. With the development of Nature and Regional Parks at Thumama and Hair, and the redevelopment of the old airport for public recreation, much of the outside pressure should be dissipated. Also once the public Desert Park in the northern wadi is complete, this should cater for outside visitors and reduce the number of families using the smaller neighbourhood parks.

More worrying in design terms is a request to fence in the Diplomatic Club to prevent casual visitors entering the Club facilities. At present low retaining walls and notices on the edge of the cliff-top public footpath are the only deterrent. Anything approaching full fencing would not only detract visually from the landscape design, it would also be alien to the original concept of a building set on the open desert plateau. Perhaps a compromise would be to increase the security around the external recreation areas. Here the retaining walls could be raised in height, reinforced by ditches and denser planting. This would keep people away from the more sensitive areas.

The original plan for the Diplomatic Quarter has been affected more strikingly by this growing sensitivity to security. Under the original plan, a population of 25,000 would reside here in five distinct neighbourhoods. In response to growing security requirements, the Government decided not to proceed with these housing areas until after the roads, servicing and social facilities had been completed. It is to be hoped that this decision can soon be rescinded and the housing development allowed to proceed. The original concept of an integrated quarter of Ar-riyadh of which the Diplomatic Community forms only a small – but important – percentage is socially and culturally sound. Meanwhile the empty spaces awaiting development are unsightly elements in an otherwise well-structured layout. Perhaps they could be treated as part of the extensive landscape area and seeded with appropriate native species.

One final thought concerns the future of Wadi Hanifah. This beautiful natural feature plays an extremely important role in the environmental quality of the Diplomatic Quarter in terms of aesthetics, recreation and climate amelioration. It is not in the ownership of the Diplomatic Quarter, however, and so any long-term changes are not in their control. It is gratifying to know that a study of the Wadi is being carried out by the ADA to encourage a long-term environmental strategy for this important landscape feature.

5

University campus design
Stirling University

In 1964 the Government, through the University Grants Commission (UGC) announced the foundation of a new Scottish university at Stirling. This location was selected after an evaluation of some seven sites in Scotland. The main criteria used in the evaluation and choice of a site were a suitable area of at least 40 ha (100 acres), in an area attractive to staff, near to industry in order to encourage pure and applied scientific research and with an existing supply of lodgings for students.

An academic plan was produced in December 1965, covering the university's size, rate of growth and recommended scope of work. It suggested three main areas of studies: the arts or humanities, the basic sciences and mathematics, and the social sciences. Students would be encouraged to build courses from any of these disciplines. This flexibility in course planning gave rise to the need for a similar flexibility in planning the teaching accommodation. The traditional concept of separate departmental buildings

gave way to that of a single block. Thus departments could grow and contract and relocate to be next to compatible disciplines.

The site chosen for the university was the Airthrey Estate, some 3km (2 miles) to the north-east of Stirling town centre. This consisted of a nineteenth-century parkland laid out by the Thomas Whites, a father-and-son practice working in the manner of Lancelot 'Capability' Brown, to complement the house designed by Robert Adam in his castellated style. The park followed the usual Brownian formula of a central water feature – in this case an artificial lochan – and a boundary belt of trees. Later picturesque additions, such as the conifer planting have been attributed to the painter Alexander Nasmyth. The natural setting for this estate is extremely dramatic, set at the southern foot of the Ochil Hills, and contained immediately to the south by Abbey Craig surmounted by the Victorian Scots Baronial tower of the Wallace Monument. Views across the flat carselands of the River Forth to the Campsie

Fells are interrupted by the silhouette of Stirling, climaxed by the Castle upon its defensive rock. Thus the site had a comparatively intimate character, contrasting with the greater and more expansive scale of the surrounding landscape.

A population of 3000 undergraduates, 500 postgraduates and 450 university staff was planned for 1975. To meet this 1975 target, a rolling financial programme was agreed with the UGC, which allowed accommodation across all functions – teaching, residences, services and administration – to proceed in unison. Thus the annual needs of the expanding university community would be met by that year's building completions. Some 20 separate building contracts were let during the seven-year construction period. The landscape input to each of these had to be co-ordinated to ensure not only a completed site at each stage of completion but also a structure that would be visually coherent and unified with the external spaces of the university campus.

THE MASTER PLAN

Robert Matthew, Johnson-Marshall & Partners, a multi-disciplinary design practice, was commissioned in January 1966 to produce a development plan for the university. This was 30 months before the first academic courses were to begin. Thus the plan had to allow for an initial multi-use building to contain all the university functions for the first three years, in addition to a longer-term plan for the entire university complex.

Three major factors influenced the form and process of the plan: the academic plan and detailed brief; the existing site; and the rolling programme of annually budgeted contracts. This last point obviously meant that building work would be continuous throughout the seven-year development phase and in several site areas at once. To minimize conflicts between construction and university operations, the building work began in the west of the site and progressed towards the east, leaving completed areas of site for the university to occupy. Thus all construction traffic used the eastern road access, and university traffic the western. By this means, the occupied campus always appeared finished during the period of development. New planting was not compromised by building work during the critical establishment period.

The site consisted of some 120 ha (300 acres) of parkland and 25 ha (62 acres) of peripheral woodland. The artificial loch provided the focus of attention at the core of the site. Land rose from this in an irregular bowl, contained by trees and landforms. In addition there were three other main spaces: to the east, south and west. These were largely separated visually from the loch area by both landform and mature tree planting. The areas around the loch and to the west were those where most of the site development occurred. The southern and eastern spaces were both divided from the loch area by low ridges. Topography in the western space varied. It contained the flattest part of the site, in the south, but rose steeply in the north. This topographical sub-division was further emphasized by the development plan, with the main entrance bisecting the two parts. Playing fields were located on the flatter area and the first university building, Pathfoot, was placed on the northern slope. This entrance zone was separated from the loch area by the embankment of the earth dam and by a tree belt. Thus the loch is screened from view until the central area itself is penetrated.

An important ingredient of the development plan was a Site Analysis Report, prepared by Edmund Hilliard, the firm's landscape architect. This clearly identified the basic natural sub-divisions of the site, their individual character and form and their visual relationships. The importance of the existing designed parkland was recognized, along with the desirabilty of integrating the new development into it.

The development plan responded to this Report by accepting the loch, major land forms and wooded area as 'essential and valuable' components in the design with a useful role to play in their changing environment. The Plan also identified the need to create a strong new landscape in the new built areas, with a transitional treatment to provide continuity between 'urban and open settings'.

The overall form proposed exploits and emphasises the natural formation of the site. The buildings rise in a shallow bowl in response to the ground form, and face each other across the loch. From many parts of the scheme the entire University will be visible at any time. Within this broad amphitheatre every element will stand revealed in its relationship to the whole.[1]

In the main these building design principles have been followed in the construction of the university. Only the initial university building, Pathfoot, the sports halls, the Principal's house, some staff housing and the boiler-house stand outwith the central space. Here the needs of the academic brief and the inherent qualities of the site are sensibly combined to produce probably the finest landscape setting for a new university in Britain. In essence, U-shaped student residences are on the south-facing slope, maximizing the limited Scottish sunshine. The teaching buildings run along the southern edge of the bowl, and the shared functions, such as library, cafeterias, shop and theatre create a central focus on a promontory reaching into the loch. Road access, car parking and services are generally kept to a peripheral loop road, with the central space around the loch free for pedestrians. Building materials were largely limited to high-quality concrete block, deep concrete fascias and dark-stained timber window frames and doors. The character was generally horizontal with the theatre fly tower the only vertical element.

Contracts were let initially for site development followed by the rolling programme of building contracts. These involved inter-disciplinary design and co-ordination between civil and mechanical engineers, architects, quantity surveyors and the landscape architect. Most of the major earth shaping was incorporated in the site development contract. This involved forming the playing-field areas, establishing the basic levels for building blocks and car parks, aligning the access roads, forming a new lochan and laying the main underground service runs.

The landscape architect was a key member of the site development team, ensuring that building locations avoided loss of existing trees, that earthwork was minimized by taking advantage of the existing landform and that building orientation took advantage of views and responded to the microclimate (Fig. 5.1).

For each year of the seven-year building programme up to three new building contracts could be let on site: a student residence, a central facility and a teaching unit. During this period, therefore, the landscape architect was involved with some 20 contracts, from concept design through building and contract supervision to establishment and maintenance. Although each building contract was supervised by separate architects, Edmund Hilliard, the landscape architect, was responsible for co-ordinating site planning aspects across the site. This involved design of all the external spaces, including car parking, footpaths, pergolas and planting.

5.1 *(Left)* **The student residences are sensitively sited on the south-facing slope above the loch, set against the backdrop of Hermitage Wood.**

5.2 *(Right)* **Planting around the car park of the residences. Bold patterns of shrubs and ground-cover plants sweep under trees, breaking up the building mass.**

THE PLANTING POLICY

The planting design of Hilliard was done in close consultation with the university Superintendent of Grounds, the late Hendry Mylne. This co-operation between the designer and manager of the landscape was recognized as important in ensuring the establishment and long-term maintenance of the project. Much of the planting contract was carried out by the university ground staff.

Five design principles guided the planting design within the general site layout. Firstly, the existing natural boundaries of landform, water and tree blocks were to be utilized and reinforced as elements of continuity threading through the site. These plantings would provide a structure to the development, 'an element of continuity, extending from afforested hillsides to the tree belts, threading through the "urban" areas; and uniting them with the parkland setting of the loch'. A second policy was that planting would progress from west to east across the site. This would co-ordinate with the building programme and minimize disturbance to establishing planting. This responded to the development plan requirement that 'a balance should be preserved between residential, teaching and communal accommodation, and between buildings, landscaping and car parking'.

A third policy decision was that colour would be provided throughout the year. This would in the main be achieved by trees through the seasonal changes in their foliage. This recognized the generally ephemeral impact of flowering trees, a short one-week season of dense colour followed by dull foliage on an often ugly form. The flowering period of some chosen species, such as the native cherry, *Prunus avium*, and the hawthorn, *Crataegus monagyna*, were consciously designed for. But these, together with autumn leaf colours were recognized as short, if memorable, seasonal incidents. The need to achieve a rapid, apparently mature effect by the planting was the fourth policy objective. This immediate impact was to be achieved by mass planting. Strong blocks of colour would result from the lower level of shrubs and ground-covers, these in the main being restricted to white and yellow flowering species (Fig. 5.2).

The final policy objective was to keep the maintenance requirements of the planting to a minimum. The overall effect was of a parkland with large areas of grass framed by buildings and bold blocks of planting. These

large areas, simple in outline, were designed for efficient grass cutting. Mowing strips were provided adjacent to buildings, and slopes too steep to mow economically were mass planted. The shrubs and ground-covers would require intensive short-term maintenance until they had grown sufficiently to suppress weed growth. The shrubs would require annual pruning to ensure continuing flowering and to restrain the more vigorous species. This demonstrates a frequent problem in planting design: the conflicting demands for immediate impact, low maintenance and floristic interest.

In principle the planting policy identified two major categories of planting, long-term shelter planting, and shorter-term ornamental planting. This latter would be seasonally attractive but would require a rolling replacement programme. Most ornamental shrubs have a maximum useful life of 15 years. After this they are usually too leggy and open in form to fulfil their original functions.

Similarly many of the ground-covers selected, particularly *Hypericum calycinum*, need annual clipping and regular subdivision if the desired compact pattern is to be achieved. These then were the stated design objectives. It is generally agreed that the completed design was a very fine marriage between built form, circulation routes and existing site values. The landscape design has always been recognized as a major contributor to the high quality of the overall design.

The close working relationship between landscape architect and university grounds superintendent has already been mentioned. As the superintendent and his staff carried out most of the planting, there was no conflict between planting, establishment and maintenance responsibilities. These were all carried out by the same personnel, working to the designs of the landscape architect. With some 20 separate building contracts in progress during the seven-year development period, the benefits of this simplified planting

contract are obvious. It also allowed the grounds superintendent to buy in small nursery stock and grow it in his own nursery for four to six years before planting it on site. This meant that more trees of a larger size could be planted within the contract budget. Also stress factors due to moving such plants were reduced, given the short length of time required to transplant them from nursery to site. This principle was also applied to many shrub species.

At the end of the development period, in 1973, the university had reached its planned student population of 3000. There was scope for expansion east of the loch to reach a target figure of 6000 undergraduates. By the mid 1970s, however, the economic climate in Britain had worsened, and the planned expansion in higher education halted, a trend that has if anything worsened since. The campus as it existed in 1973 is thus a useful baseline against which to judge subsequent changes.

THE 1973 DEVELOPMENT

The main core of the university was within the natural bowl around the already existing loch, with residences on the north shore, the main teaching buildings on the southern lip of the bowl and the library and social facilities on the southern loch side. To the north, the steeply-treed slopes of Hermitage Wood form a backcloth to the residences and extend fingers of shelter belts into and around the site. One such belt reinforces the landform to

create the visual boundary on the west between the core area and the playing fields. The Principal's house sits on a rocky plateau, within the Hermitage Wood. Eastwards, the original parkland character continues forming an appropriate setting for Aithrey Castle, and extends to the ground-level boundary of the peripheral tree belt. Above and beyond this the eye is carried by the sweep of Hermitage Wood up to the open

slopes of the Ochil Hills. On the south the edge of the central bowl is defined by a slight rise, topped by a line of ancient oak trees. This ridge hides a sizeable area of university land, kept in agricultural use at this stage of development, as is other peripheral land. Towering above this ridge is Abbey Craig, a wooded volcanic plug, dramatically crowned by the tower of the Wallace Monument.

Entrance to the university is from the west,

breaking through the original stone boundary wall and tree belt. The entrance space lies outside the central bowl and is defined by peripheral tree belts. It falls into two parts: to the south the sports hall and playing fields, to the north the Pathfoot Building. Service facilities, such as the boiler house and the plant nursery, lie to the east of the central space.

The initial impression of the 1973 development was of a mature parkland, within which a new set of functions happily sat. The relationships between landform, water and vegetation, and roads and buildings were very carefully and well resolved. Original spatial divisions were cleverly utilized to contain buildings, car parks and roads. The unity of architectural form and materials was matched by similar bold landscape treatments. This seemingly natural outcome, however, was the result of much thought and attention to detail. Landform was adjusted, particularly for the playing fields, roads and car parks.

In order to service the central social facilities, a causeway was built across an arm of the loch. This left a small pond or lochan, which was used as a focus for the central dining areas. Lawns sweep down to the water's edge, with sculpture and specimen trees between (Fig. 5.3). In contrast the edge of the original loch was treated in a natural manner, with water edge species such as *Typha latifolia* and *Cornus alba*, backed by taller shrubs such as *Crataegus monagyna* and *Symphoricarpus alba*. The loch was intended to act as a teaching and sporting resource for the university, with potential academic benefit to the Botany and Marine Biology Departments. Limited sailing and canoeing were also catered for. Indeed it has been suggested that the height of the pedestrian bridge connecting the residences to the central facilities was established by the clearance required for the mast of the Principal's sailing dinghy.

The natural approach to planting was applied to the larger blocks of planting and to Hermitage Wood. The maintenance of some 7 ha (17½ acres) of woodland was carried out by a contractor. The landscape architect provided a management plan, with guidelines on timing, planting and species. The species were mainly hardwoods, supplemented by some conifers to give winter shelter.

Where the broad belts of planting approached the buildings, their scale was reduced to species such as *Sorbus intermedia, S. Aucuparia* and *Betula sp*. Existing trees near buildings and road alignments were wherever possible retained. These large trees were a major factor in successfully relating the development to the site by establishing an instant maturity. Mass planting alongside the roads and around and within the car parks also contributed to this early integration.

Each residential block had its own parking area. However, the teaching and central areas were served by a single area to the west of the teaching building. Here the designer skilfully manipulated the slope by introducing retaining walls topped with planting beds both to break up the space into smaller areas and to control the circulation – of vehicles and pedestrians. Small trees rose out of mass shrub planting and pendulous ground-cover, which clothed the face of the retaining walls.

Vehicular access to the central area for servicing and setting down people is restricted to the Queen's Court. Here the mass planting of small trees, shrubs and ground-covers was concentrated on slopes and in the central roundabout. This reinforced the basic shape of the space, articulated the circulation pattern and visually connected the court to the adjacent spaces. *Cotoneaster sp., Hedera sp.* and *Juniperus sp.* were the main ground-cover plants, with *Prunus avium* and *Sorbus aucuparia* as the main trees. This simple treatment effectively counterbalanced the necessarily large areas of road and paving and broke up the horizontal elevational pattern of the enclosing buildings.

The central buildings sit some 5m (16.5ft) above the main loch, with no direct connection to it. Pedestrian movement between these buildings and the residences is by a horizontal footbridge, which continues at the same level to the teaching buildings. This circulation system was designed as a varied and stimulating sequence of spaces, articulating relationships between the varied university activities and communities and between the external and internal environments. Thus the more personal student areas – the residences – were given a visual and physical buffer from the working and social areas. In contrast, these areas were more closely related, connected by an enclosed bridge or corridor. Spaces were largely introverted as internal streets, social spaces or courtyards.

As mentioned previously, only the eating areas open out to the landscape where they relate to the newly-created pond. From the glazed bridge between teaching and central areas there are views into both the Queen's

5.3 **The central facilities, seen across the smaller loch.**

5.4 *(Right)* **Original planting in an internal courtyard of the teaching buildings. It has not been regularly pruned and is now beginning to lose the original form and mass.**

Court and the new pond but no physical connections. The four internal courtyards within the Cotterell (Teaching) Building were each treated in a simple but distinctive manner. The central courtyard is an important arrival and orientation space. To meet the demands of heavy pedestrian use, much of it was paved. A pattern was established by a 2.5m (8ft) grid of granite setts, infilled by 16 square concrete paving slabs. The ends of this courtyard, outside the circulation area, were planted. Here the basic principle of boldly massing small trees, shrubs and ground-cover was again followed. Species such as *Cotoneaster sp.*, *Gaultheria shallon* and *Juniperous sabine* were supplemented here by a drift of azalea in the eastern bed. A large Scots pine, *Pinus sylvestris*, was also included as a strong vertical element.

Circulation in the remaining three courtyards was concentrated mainly along the southern edge. This allowed these areas to be more freely planted, with less paving. In two of the courtyards grass was used as the surface outwith the planting beds. In the most easterly courtyard, three circular planting beds were placed within the grass sward. The aim was to create three dense domes of vegetation rising through layers of ground-cover and shrubs to a canopy of trees. Although mainly deciduous, a core of evergreen plants, such as *Tsuga heterophylla*, *Ligustrum vulagare*, *Taxus baccata* and *Vinca minor*, aimed to retain this vegetative density throughout the dormant season (Fig. 5.4).

In the remaining two courtyards, three diagonal paths were established, dividing each area into three planting beds. The paths were surfaced in gravel in the western space

and grassed in the other. In all courtyards, 300-mm (12-in.) wide mowing strips of river-washed gravel were laid alongside the buildings. This was to keep maintenance in the grassed areas to a minimum and to define the edge of each space in a similar manner, giving an element of continuity with the buildings. The mass-planting principle was again followed in these last two areas. However, each was given a separate character by mixing eight different varieties of *Erica sp.* in the eastern one and six varieties of dwarf *Rhododendron sp.* in the other.

Although a greater variety of plant material was used here than in the larger parkland spaces, each was given a clear structure and focus, with plant species used to reinforce the desired effect. The areas were mainly seen as visual extensions of the surrounding rooms, places to be looked into rather than walked through – although this was also allowed for to varying degrees.

Enclosed external spaces were also a feature of the Pathfoot building. This building was designed and constructed in advance of the development plan. It housed all the teaching administration, and social facilities for the first few years of the institution's life while the development plan was being designed and constructed. The building is located on the slope above the main entrance to the campus. This position was chosen as it had convenient access, would not restrict the main development still to be planned, and would in turn not be disturbed by building work on that development.

PATHFOOT

In plan Pathfoot consists of six parallel blocks with connecting links set at right angles. The blocks lie across the contours of the sloping site and the linking corridors subdivide the spaces between the blocks into a series of courtyards, alternately flat or sloping as they progress up the slope from the main entrance. The level courtyards were developed as visual and useful extensions to the adjoining corridors and rooms, whilst the sloping area acted more as light wells. Servicing was at the top of the site, where the kitchen and dining facilities were located, with the main car parking by the lower, main entrance. The access road to this entrance and the car park sliced rather unhappily across the slope. This was emphasized by the strong horizontal lines of the building. A steep flight of steps led pedestrians from the main campus entrance to the building.

The late Frank Clark was landscape consultant for the Pathfoot contract. His design of the courtyards reflects the character of the building, creating simple outside rooms

on the level areas and densely planting the slopes to combat possible erosion and to reduce maintenance. In the 10 × 19 m (33 × 62ft) courtyards simple rectangles of paving or grass were complemented by a few carefully chosen and located low shrubs or small trees. The courtyards furthest from the main access were simply grassed and had a group of three trees. Species of shrubs used were *Rhododendron sp., Erica sp., Gaultheria shallon, Betula pendula.* The geometry of the design responded to the form of the space and the character of the enclosing building (Fig. 5.5). Planting on the slopes was of *Juniperus sp.* As a later part of the development plan these slopes were reinforced with *Dryopteris sp., Erica sp.* and *Vaccinium sp.* Trees and mass planting of

Hypericum calycinum were drifted into the open ends of the eastern courtyards to link the building into the rest of the site.

The playing fields – an area covering some 9 ha (22.5 acres) – were developed on the western boundary of the site. They lie within a self-contained land unit, enclosed by both landform and tree belts. The associated buildings are well integrated with the contours to lessen their bulk and visual impact. Maintenance was a major determinant in the design of the landscape. This was reflected in the use of mass planting balanced by sweeping, easily-mown grass areas. In general all steep slopes were shrub planted, mowing strips were provided where grass met vertical walls, and individual trees in grass were kept to a minimum. Shrub

species were restricted to those requiring simple annual pruning. The landscape architect and the grounds superintendent worked closely together during the design and contract stage, and their working relationship has been recognized as a model of its kind. As the university grounds staff carried out much of the planting programme as well as the maintenance, there were none of the usual conflicts that arise when these operations are carried out by two separate organizations. By organizing his workforce to have responsibility for the planting and establishment of the campus planting, Hendry Mylne captured their interest in the process, and there was a seamless transition from site works through to a successfully working university campus.

5.5 **The original design for the internal courtyards at the Pathfoot Building was a simple play of horizontal paving and grass against a few carefully composed plants. The geometric pattern reflected the building elevations.**

THE CHANGING SITUATION

This success was shown in the interest taken in the new university by architectural critics, horticulturists and the public. It rapidly became popular as a location for conferences, summer schools and family holiday accommodation, largely due to the landscape setting. For various reasons the landscape has had to adapt to changes, in the form of both new functions and in management. Some of these the development plan has been robust or flexible enough to accommodate. Others are more damaging, and threaten the coherence and clarity of the original concept.

Attitudes to tertiary education have radically changed since the early 1960s, when

the Robbins Report predicted seemingly unlimited growth in the sector. As Stirling University reached the end of its projected Phase 2 development in 1973, economic restraints were already threatening the original projected Phase 3 expansion to an undergraduate population of 6000. The projected expansions did not happen, and by 1988 the aim was for a population of 3000. A major consequence of this was that the university had more land than it needed for these reduced academic circumstances. At the same time, together with other British universities, it was being encouraged by Government to seek revenue-earning

partnerships with industry and business. This is a phenomenon common in the developed world and has spawned Innovation, Business and Technology Parks, which endeavour to achieve entrepreneurial benefits from academic research. Stirling has now developed three new areas of the campus for different purposes. These are a manufacturing laboratory originally for Wang Computers, an Innovation Park and a Business Centre. All three are located in the southern edge of the campus, as discrete enterprises (Fig. 5.6 and 5.7).

IIIIIIIIIIII	Campus boundary	7.	Central facilities
– – –	Forrest/Mylne Walks	8.	Teaching
1.	Pathfoot	9.	Sports hall
2.	Residences	10.	Playing fields
3.	Staff	11.	Business centre
4.	Greenhouses/nursery	12.	Innovation park
5.	Airthrey Castle	13.	Maintenance
6.	Golf course	14.	Wang Laboratories

5.6   **Stirling University campus.**

5.7   *(Right)* **Stirling University campus from Abbey Craig. The broad scale siting of the new Business Centre (left) and the Innovation Park (right) complements the aims of the original master plan. However, they lack a clear planting structure to tie them into the existing planting and land form.**

5.8 *(Left)* **These single storey postgraduate residences are absorbed and integrated into the maturing campus landscape.**

5.9 *(Right)* **The new Business Centre borrows nothing in form or materials from the original university buildings.**

On the parkland immediately south of Airthrey Castle the University has itself developed a nine-hole golf course. This is used by both the university community and the general public. It is a popular and money-earning facility. Two interpretative walks have also been developed, one to display plants collected by George Forrest, the other in memory of Hendry Mylne. Land next to the university has been developed by the Gardeners' Memorial Trust, in memory of

gardeners everywhere. This is supervised by the St Andrew's Botanical Gardens.

To meet a demand for accommodation for senior students, the university in 1981 negotiated a design-and-build contract with a local firm of builders. Ten units were built on the north-west corner of the campus, between the residences and the Pathfoot building. These were single-storey timber buildings from the contractor's standard range of self-catering holiday cabins. Architecturally these

are completely alien, in scale, character and materials, to the original residences. They also lie outside the service road, a policy broken by only one of the initial blocks. However, they are carefully sited within the existing trees, do not intrude visually and so are not seen against the earlier buildings. They are extremely popular with the student occupants (Fig. 5.8).

THE BUSINESS CENTRE

The Business Centre is run as a separate operation, providing a hotel standard of service for people attending residential courses (Fig. 5.9). These courses are run as commercial, revenue-earning enterprises. The building was consciously designed to contrast with the existing teaching blocks as a low-slung Y-shaped building, clad in brown brick and with a concrete-tiled pitched roof. The architect wished to introduce colour onto the site to enliven what he described as the drab greys of the university. His original idea to have a red-tiled roof was rejected by the local Planning Department. So the design, although different, is restrained in colour and form.

The site for the Business Centre lies south of the teaching building, across a slight ridge. This is topped by a line of ancient oak trees. To the south the land rises quite steeply to a belt of trees, which sweeps around the site to form the western boundary. A few groups of mature oaks filter the view towards the east, which carries on in the direction of the Innovation Park, until blocked by another belt of trees. Above this intermediate southern boundary rises Abbey Craig, topped by the Wallace Monument. The architect has deliberately used this as a focus for the building, opening the views from the social areas and the bedrooms towards this feature. The building itself sits on a level platform, cut into the regraded slope. Vehicular access is from the campus through the main car park. Parking for the building lies along the north, on either side of the main entrance. A service yard on the west gable is adjacent to the kitchen area.

As a result of the general physical and visual containment of the site, this new building does not intrude into the general university campus. Although contrasting in form, materials and scale with the existing buildings, it is in itself a simple and pleasant design, which relates successfully to its setting. It is regrettable, however, that very little of the budget has been spent on planting, and that which has, was used merely to decorate the building. Beds of low shrubs and ground-cover plants are located next to the building and around the car park. Little use has been made of ground-modelling or bold tree and shrub planting to settle the car parking and access road into the existing land form or to tie the building more harmoniously into the setting. The bold, simple design approach of the development plan is lacking.

THE INNOVATION PARK

This same tentative, after-the-event approach to planting is also apparent at the first two buildings occupying the Innovation Park (Fig. 5.10). This is a joint venture between the university, the Scottish Development Agency (SDA) and the Central Regional Council. The aim is to provide plots, in a variety of sizes, to companies keen to engage in research and development projects, with access to the university's academic and research facilities. As the first phase, a full road system with car parking was installed, together with full servicing of gas, electricity, water and drainage.

'Comprehensive landscaping' was also listed as a feature in the brochure advertising the project.[2] At site development stage this seems to have consisted of a featureless spoil heap heavily planted with seedling trees and shrubs and a scattering of larger deciduous trees along the access road. This infrastructure stage was implemented by the SDA, and maintenance – mainly grass cutting – is carried out by the university's grounds staff. As with the Business Centre, the site, some 5.5 ha (13.75 acres) in area, is visually separated from the main university complex. It fronts the Hillfoot Road, the southern campus boundary, and is enclosed on the other three sides by trees of varying density – on the west the site merges imperceptibly between clumps of trees with the Business Centre.

The site is approached from the Hillfoot Road, using the upgraded university service access. From this, three spur roads initially subdivide the site, with the site boundary set back from the public road to retain a rural character. The new ground modelling for this phase seems in parts unnecessarily crude. Steep, unnatural embankments blend poorly with the new roads and the existing land form. Planting seems similarly uncoordinated, with little attention paid to developing a new structure from the existing mature trees on site. The crudely-formed central mound is exuberantly planted with a range of deciduous trees, with, however, little apparent thought of the bare winter effect. This boldness contrasts strongly with the widely-spaced standard trees, flanking the access road. These lack unity, form or clarity and fail to give any impact or character to the largely-undeveloped site, which has to depend largely on the quality of the existing landscape to impress prospective developers.

Two sites have been developed, as semi-speculative ventures, by Scottish Metropolitan Property Plc. The Alpha and Beta Centres provide rentable sites of flexible accommodation for research and development, with shared administrative and catering facilities. Each centre consists of two slightly off-set blocks, linked by the entrance and common service areas. Although small in scale the buildings relate crudely to the site, and the car parking areas tend to dominate. The whole development is rather squeezed between the site boundary and the spur road, which is generally at a higher level. The rather uninteresting and timid planting tends to emphasize this poor relationship between building, car parking and road. At present the Innovation Park is unattractive, its form and structure need to be clarified and strengthened and the visual impact of the setting for these initial buildings reduced.

5.10 **The recent Innovation Park is well located on the southern edge of the campus. Unfortunately the first buildings are rather crudely sited in relation to landform and the new planting lacks a definite character or structure.**

WANG LABORATORIES

Wang Laboratories UK have located their European manufacturing plant on the eastern edge of the campus, between the Hillfoot Road and the loch (Fig. 5.11). Two of a possible three building phases are now complete. Although the company wanted to be on the campus, they required a separately-serviced site with its own entrance. The site had a complex topography, being essentially a saddle between two land formations. The eastern edge of the site was a steep wooded slope, falling sharply to the public road.

The development brief required a large industrial building combined with a suite of offices and an extensive area of vehicle parking. Major earthmoving was necessary to accommodate all these elements on site, and the result is rather crude and relates poorly to the existing landform. The building itself picks up elements from the university development particularly the use of a deep exposed aggregate concrete fascia. From within the campus the building seems at present fairly effectively integrated. Existing landform and planting mask the bulk of the built form, and the visible fragments appear in scale and harmony with the setting. Within the Wang site, however, the building often sits poorly in its location. There is no sense of arrival to the main public entrance and the narrow grassed space falls sharply away from the dominant roadway, leading the eye rapidly past the building. This channelling effect is reinforced by the low, clipped shrub beds, severely contained between building and road. The vehicle park overpowers the southern area, and again the ground modelling is crude and angular. A strong belt of existing trees along the site boundary gives good shelter to this area, but no attempt has been made to extend parts of this into the parking area to break across the saddle of ground and become a major new element in the campus landscape. Unless the site works and planting are handled with more sensitivity than has been shown so far, the effect will be discordant. (During production of this book Wang have closed their enterprise at Stirling.)

None of these recent building developments shows good landscape design qualities when compared with the original bold concepts of the development plan. However, their impact on the rest of the campus is negligible. This is due to their general siting, within discrete pockets of ground largely contained by landform, and tree belts. It demonstrates the correctness of the development plan's decision to concentrate the university buildings in the central bowl around the loch, leaving the peripheral areas free for alternative uses. A more dispersed layout would have compromised the later options. The developments and changes that have had the greatest detrimental effects on the campus come from changes in open space functions, and in planting design and management.

5.11 **This new manufacturing building is placed in a discrete landscape unit. There is, however, little attention to detailed landscape issues, shown, for instance, by the large, open parking area.**

THE GOLF COURSE

A major change has taken place in the original parkland south of Airthrey Castle. This is the site of the nine-hole golf course designed by Hendry Mylne and constructed with a Youth Training Scheme labour force. In order to accommodate the required tees, fairways and greens the park has been criss-crossed with lines of trees and pockmarked with crudely-levelled tee areas (Fig. 5.12). Each line of separating trees consists of a different species, widely spaced to facilitate grass cutting. The former sweeping sward, punctuated by graceful clumps of trees, is now an uncoordinated discordant mess, with no logical spatial form or sequence. Parkland has frequently been successfully converted to golf course, but more cognisance has been given to the parkland qualities – with greater spaces, denser tree planting and careful attention to the balance between solid and void, and between new and existing landform. A golf course on this site needs more land so that the lines of the fairways can be relaxed to adjust to the subtleties of the landscape.

This approach to planting has unfortunately been applied to other parts of the broader campus, particularly on the southern loch shore, east of the pedestrian bridge. Again trees are widely spaced and uncoordinated in terms of species. The effect is very weak, with no structure, focus or character. Isolated conical conifers stand rigidly in lawns next to oval shrub beds reminiscent of the worst municipal parks. This is the Hendry Mylne Walk, created to

remember one of the key persons responsible for establishing the campus landscape – a design of boldly massed trees, shrubs and ground-covers. It seems an inappropriate memorial (Fig. 5.13).

5.12 (Above) **The recent golf course intrudes into the rolling parkland around Airthrey Castle. Too many varieties of tree are used in the belts separating the fairways. Plastic grass tee areas and protective hedges of golden Leyland cypresses bring extra clutter to this sadly mutilated part of the campus.**

5.13 (Right) **Recent planting along the Hendry Mylne Walk is out of character with the rest of the campus. Island beds and widely-spaced individual tree specimens give too much variety and detract from the overall unity of the site.**

CHANGES TO THE COURTYARDS

The initial planting design is also being severely altered in the courtyards, at both Pathfoot and the teaching buildings. In both areas much of the planting has grown beyond the scale of the space and requires sensitive management. Regrettably those which have been treated have undergone major and radical alterations. At Pathfoot, one courtyard has been completely redesigned as a quasi-Japanese garden (Fig. 5.14). Free form beds are edged with crudely-cut paving stones, the rest of the area put down to gravel and inconsequential boulders. The careful blending of courtyard design to building design has gone, replaced by a quirky and poorly-detailed layout. The whole effect jars.

At the teaching buildings, the central courtyard has experienced the most change. All that seems to remain of the original design are the paving and the Scots pine tree (Fig. 5.15). The remaining planting has been swept away, replaced by suburban rockeries complete with pools and dwarf conifers. A designed planting structure has been replaced by a jumble of individual plant species, with no coherent pattern, form or texture governing their selection. In two of the other courtyards, much of the original ground cover and shrub planting has been removed and replaced with a wider range of less complementary species. Again dwarf conifers introduce an inappropriate scale and form to the design, and the strong multi-layered effect of the original scheme has given way to more openness and emphasis on individual plants.

It has already been emphasized that previously this was an example of landscape designer and landscape manager working together from the outset of the project to ensure that the two meshed together to ensure a coherent good quality design that could be maintained within an economic budget and with a reasonable workforce. How then has this deterioration in the quality of the campus landscape come about? There are at least three apparent reasons.

Firstly, changing economic forces have decreased the budget for grounds maintenance, with a consequent shortfall in labour force and equipment. At the end of the development period the maintenance staff were some 20 in number; this has been reduced to 13. Although the overall budget has been maintained at a constant level, rising labour and material costs mean that this has in effect been decreasing. This in turn has led to the grounds budget seeking new funding sources. The golf course is one example, another is plant sales from the university nursery. To increase these, more popular and readily-saleable species have been propagated and these are also now being planted within the campus.

A second important factor contributing to loss of the original landscape quality can be attributed to Hendry Mylne's working practice, as described by his successor, Jim Struthers, who was formerly his chief assistant. Mylne did not have a documented management plan. He issued instructions personally to his supervisors on a weekly, sometimes even a daily basis. The supervisors

5.14 (Right) Several courtyards at Pathfoot have been redesigned using crude free-form shapes and poorly-resolved paving elements. The resulting pattern bears no relation to the adjacent building form.

5.15 (Above) The courtyard of the central teaching building has been replanted, with the emphasis on individual plant specimens. The result is too rich and busy, lacking the simple, clear form and mass of the original scheme.

the population was about 800, reaching a peak of 5000 within the decade. A narrow-gauge railway reached the town in 1890, and continued operations until 1951.

By 1953 the mining operations were largely controlled by the Idarado Mining Company, who radically restructured and mechanized their processes. Their underground shafts and tunnels are rumoured to extend to Ouray, a town some 15km (10 miles) to the north-east. Two large tailing ponds east of the town are the most visible legacy of this period of development. By the 1960s, however, most mines were closed or mothballed, and the population of Telluride had declined to some 500 persons.[1]

Coinciding with this decline was the discovery of the scenic qualities of the area by outsiders, and there was a minor influx of people seeking a rural, alternative lifestyle. These are still referred to locally as 'the hippies'.[2] Local enterprises evolved to cater for summer visitors, such as jeep trips into the rugged mountains, catering and limited accommodation. The historic and urban design quality of the settlement was recognized in 1964, when Telluride was declared a National Historic Landmark. As a result of this, existing buildings are protected, and the height, density and materials of new ones are controlled.

This seemingly bucolic lifestyle was changed in 1969 by the intervention of a Californian lawyer and entrepreneur, Joe Zoline. He had acquired some 1400 ha (3500 acres) of ranch- and forest-land south-west of the town, as well as blocks within Telluride. His dream was to develop the year-round recreation potential of the area, based on winter downhill skiing and summer outdoor pursuits. By 1972 he had invested some £5 million in the form of ski lifts and runs, and condominium development in the town. The master plan that he commissioned and how it has evolved subsequently will be the main focus of this chapter.

THE PLAN AND IMPLEMENTATION

In 1979 Zoline sold the majority of his property to another developer, Ron Allred. He has, however, retained one holding on the extreme west of the site. When Allred took over there were no major facilities on the ski slopes, apart from the lifts: access to the runs was by two ski lifts from the town. In order to make a return on his investment he concentrated on establishing the major base, or village, recommended by the 1970 master plan and reinforcing the summer uses. This was largely to stimulate and widen the market for the ancillary real estate, the sales of which represented the return on his capital. To direct this development, a regional plan was drawn up in 1979, which brought together all the major landowners, developers, the Town and County authorities, and the National Forest services. This plan was further updated in 1989.

This brief outline of the changes to Telluride over the last 100 years, and particularly in the last 20, provides a background against which to consider the latest proposals to develop the area for recreation. It establishes that this is a dynamic landscape that has been exploited by humankind since the discovery of precious metals. Earth has been shifted, forests cut down, water courses altered. The vegetation cover today is secondary growth, kept in an unnatural balance of meadow, aspen and spruce only by grazing activities. Thus the changes instigated by Zoline and continued by Allred are not taking place in pristine, natural scenery, beautiful as it is.

The role of a landscape designer in these circumstances is to recognize the intrinsic qualities of the landscape and attempt to shape the development in a form that does not compromise these. The aim should be to ensure a good fit between new and existing forms, so that ski runs, golf courses, roads and buildings are sympathetic to landform and geology, water courses, vegetation and the overall view. From a social science point of view it is important also to ensure a continuing livelihood for a community threatened with job losses from closing mines.

THE FEASIBILITY STUDY

When Joe Zoline began to develop the mountain area of Telluride, he required a permit from the US National Forest Service, since much of the skiing area extends into their land. A feasibility study was prepared in 1970 in order to obtain this permission.[3] Professor Ronald Lovinger of Oregon University was landscape consultant to the design team. His employment was largely at the insistence of the Forest Service, who were aware of the visual and environmental damage that such a development could cause in this fragile landscape. The US Forest Service thus exert a strong influence over local land use.

One of the stated objectives of the design team was to examine the capabilities and capacities for development of the site so as to reinforce and preserve the unique value of the existing apparently natural landscape.[4] This was achieved by studying the natural systems which have determined the present landscape, understanding how these currently function and evaluating how they would be affected by the proposed development. The key natural systems identified were geology, hydrology, wildlife, vegetation, orientation and slopes, and climate (particularly high winds and avalanche areas). These were evaluated, individually and in combination, to find the best fit between scale of development and conservation of the natural systems.

In geological terms, the Rocky Mountain system is a young formation, still in the process of major erosion from water and ice.

The local San Juan Mountains consist mainly of the initial layers of sedimentary rocks thrust upwards by intrusive igneous granitic formations. The main layers of sediment were hard conglomerate and sandstone, sandwiching softer shales. Landslides occurred 15,000–30,000 years ago when the shales were eroded, carrying the harder formations with them. In these areas of historic landslip, it is important that the natural drainage pattern is not interfered with and that there is minimal disturbance to the vegetation. Where such change has occurred in the form of irrigation ditches, ground slump, tree loss and erosion have followed.

Four geological zones were identified, ranging from stable to unstable rock formations. Thus areas with most resistant rock formations could sustain large-scale developments; glacial moraines were deemed suitable for medium-scale construction; the historical landslip area was suitable only for lightweight constructions and no building was possible in the areas of unstable rocks, such as tallus and shales.

There are also four distinct habitats in the region: the alpine mountain region (which does not occur within the site boundaries); the spruce forests – the natural climax species; the groves of aspen, which extend in swathes up to 3300m (10,700ft) and the meadow areas, mainly along the river valleys and in clearings in the woodlands. These meadows, rich in grasses and wildflowers, are dependent for their survival on grazing animals. At the time of the feasibility study, overgrazing was occurring, limiting the richness of species. However, a balance must be struck, for if the grazing is reduced too much the spruce will recolonize and the diversity of habitat and wildlife, scenery and recreational opportunity will be reduced. The local wildlife is also dependent on the varied water bodies – the small streams, wet lands, ponds and lakes. The interdependence of water, vegetation and wildlife must be recognized if these resources are to be maintained for the continued well-being of the area.

The factors of orientation and slope have a major bearing on the suitability of the area for downhill skiing. Slopes facing north and east retain snow longer, whilst buildings are best located on the sunnier areas facing south and west. A ski resort hopes to attract all levels of skiers, from beginners to international experts and each of these require runs related to their experience and skill, reflected in the degree of slope. Beginners need wide, gentle slopes whilst experts welcome the challenge of near vertical drops through the forest. But for all skiers safety is paramount. Locations prone to high winds that can close down lifts and drift snow must be avoided. Areas prone to avalanches should be excluded from ski slopes and trails.

These, then, are the natural factors that have shaped the development of Telluride. The designers' next task was to define those activities that seemed compatible with the natural attributes and would cause least interference with the processes of nature. Four classes of activity evolved: winter recreation; summer recreation; all-year-around recreation; and commercial activities.

The first three relate mainly to outdoor pursuits, such as skiing, camping and hiking, and hunting and fishing. The fourth consists mainly of the eating, living, shopping and entertainment facilities necessary for users of

the first three ranges of activities. Each class of activity places special demands on the environment in terms of linear trails, access routes and systems, and various forms and density of building.

THE SKI TRAILS

Downhill skiing was seen as the major activity within the development. The design of the ski trails and their associated lifts was thus the major determinant of the development concept. All buildings and structures were to enhance rather than modify the site and skiing experience. A French skiing consultant, Emile Allais, skied the area in March 1970. His preliminary recommendations were analysed and adjusted with regard to the natural systems and the topography and can be tabulated thus:

Trails were tested to ensure each matched a particular level of skiing ability. They were also adjusted to relate better to natural features in the landscape. The termination points of these trails and their lifts were obvious locations for associated developments, such as restaurants, shops and accommodation. All potential building locations were also evaluated against the natural features:

This stage of the design process is summarized in the development diagram (Fig. 6.1). This illustrates the structure of the area and how various zones of development respond to this factor. It brings together the development facilities and the natural site assets and synthesizes these to establish a best fit between all elements. The dominant feature within the development site is the ridge system, comprising Coonskin Mountain, Gold Hill and Bald Mountain, which encloses the site on three sides. This ridge offers spectacular views, defines the boundaries of the area and gives it a physical unity. The design therefore aims to locate all major facilities in a positive relationship with the ridge so as to strengthen and reinforce this dominant element. Six separate development zones are identified. Zones 1–4 are the key skiing areas, having north-facing slopes of suitable gradients (7 per cent – 60+ per cent). These slopes will be serviced by two low-level developments: the new Base Development and the Town Terminus at Telluride. (This is the only element not contained by the ridge.) Three mountain lodges on each of the ridge peaks will provide high-level facilities.

The non-skiable meadows – Zones 5 and 6 –

Natural System	Ski trails and lifts
Hydrology and topography	Landform, drainage and conservation of water systems
Vegetation	Snow retaining characteristics Location of clearings
Orientation	North and East facing areas
Slopes	Skiing ability
High wind/avalanche	Avoidance of potential hazards

Table 6.1: *Effect of natural systems on design of ski trails and uplift* (*Source:* Telluride Feasibility Study)

Natural System	Building
Geology	Ground stability
Hydrology	Drainage and conservation of water systems
Vegetation	Location of clearings
Orientation	South and West facing areas
Slope	Type of structure
High wind/avalanche	Avoidance of potential hazards

Table 6.2: *Effect of natural systems on building location and design* (*Source:* Telluride Feasibility Study)

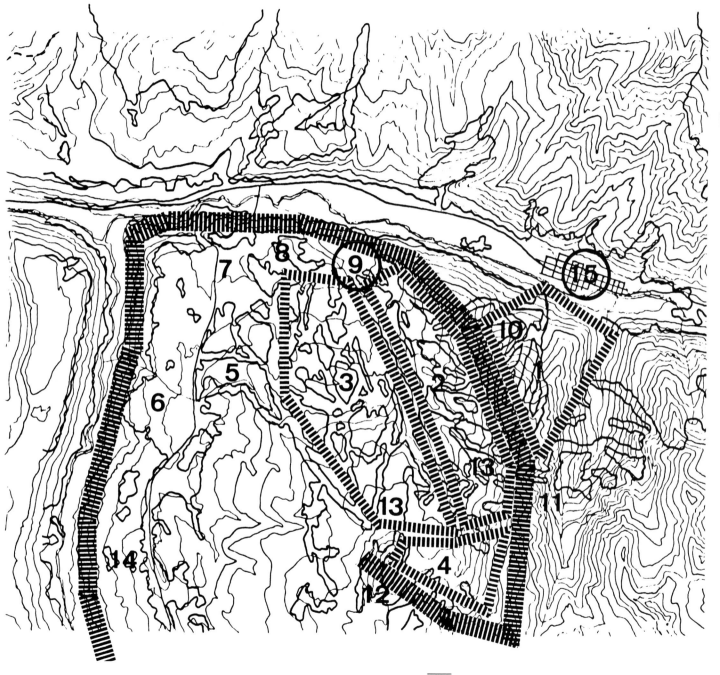

|||||| Ridge line
||||||| Ski slopes

1. Competition
2. Prospect East
3. Prospect West
4. Prospect Basin

Accommodation

5. Meadow East
6. Meadow West
7. The Entrance
8. The Ranch
9. The Base
10. Coonskin Mt.
11. Goldhill
12. Bald Mt.
13. Movable structures
14. Camping
15. Town terminus

6.1 The development diagram from the 1970 feasibility study for Telluride. (*MacAllister.*)

will be used mainly for accommodation. These will include medium-density condominiums, ranch dwellings and camping facilities. The largest development will be the Base Development and the Meadow Condominiums, located on or near the geologically-stable ridge. The smaller, lightweight units are located on the less stable geological area, in Zone 5. 'Thus,' claims the feasibility study, 'that part of the area which geologically and visually can best support new elements will receive them, while the more delicate areas will be preserved in an almost untouched state.'

The designers perceived Telluride as an exceptional development opportunity, citing its location – near many national parks, such as the Grand Canyon and Mesa Verde – and wildlife areas, the inherent beauty of the site itself, and the outstanding ski terrain and potential for summer activities. Their plan proposed a family-oriented year-round resort, similar in scale to French Alpine resorts, such as Courcheval and Tignes, with skiing as the major focus. The concentration of facilities in small areas retains the maximum amount of open land, preserves the natural beauty of the site, increases opportunities for social contacts and leads to more economic development.

They recognized that their plan was only a guide for future development, not a detailed prescription: ' . . . the Development Plan has been designed to be responsible to social, environmental and economic needs. As Telluride grows, other needs and demands will emerge, and this plan will be able to serve them. Only a flexible and responsive plan can hope to meet the changing recreational markets of the seventies and eighties and to fulfil the opportunity and challenge that is Telluride.'[5] Almost 20 years after the preparation of the feasibility study, from which this statement comes, it is a valuable exercise to examine the physical reality of Telluride, and evaluate how successfully it has achieved the original goals.

PHASE ONE

The feasibility study provided a Phase One development plan (Fig. 6.2). This envisaged the new entrance orientation point; road access from Route 145; base accommodation for 500 people plus 12,800 sq.m (142,000 sq.ft) of commercial and service facilities; and an initial ski lift and ski-trail development along the ridge and Prospect East. In addition to the new base village, the intention was to revitalize the town of Telluride by sympathetic infill with facilities to support the skiing activities. To finance this initial phase, the East Meadow Housing sites were sold off by Joe Zoline to other developers (Fig. 6.3).

Through a combination of small entrepreneurs and investment by Zoline, the old town was revitalized and the first stage of the Town Terminus and the Mountain Base constructed (Fig. 6.4). Five lifts were built. Trails were sympathetically manipulated by connecting existing fire breaks, logging trails and natural glades. This kept tree-felling to a minimum. The work was carried out using the landscape architect's conceptual drawings for guidance (Figs. 6.5 and 6.6). A team consisting of the landscape architect, a local representative of the development company and the district ranger from the National Forest Service walked the trails during the summer using the fall-line established by Allais as centre line. They agreed on the width and line of trails, and marked all trees to be felled. They also agreed a working plan of operations to ensure that all scrub and timber was properly disposed of and that no erosion problems would result from trail clearance. This process continued over three years, adjusting the edges of the trails each year.

Thus when Ron Allred took over the development in 1979 he inherited winter sports lifts and trails but little in the way of back-up facilities, particularly on the mountain. Although some 40 per cent of skiers used the Mountain Base lift, this had only basic facilities, and there were no restaurants on the mountain. Meanwhile ski-lift technology had progressed, so that the original tows were slow and out of date. The need now was to establish a fully-serviced base on the mountain, not to replace Telluride but to complement it. Stimulated by Zoline's

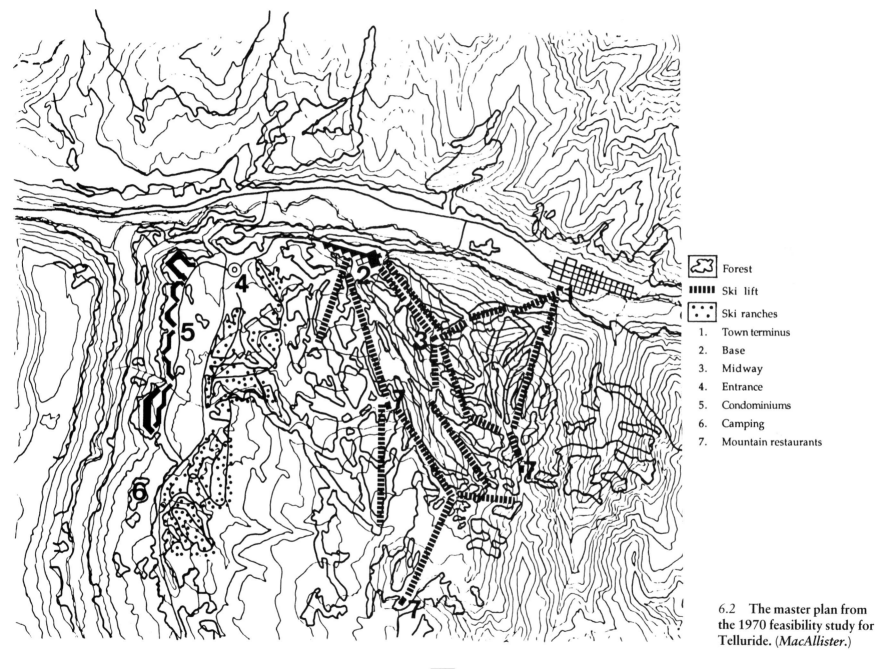

Forest

Ski lift

Ski ranches

1. Town terminus
2. Base
3. Midway
4. Entrance
5. Condominiums
6. Camping
7. Mountain restaurants

6.2 **The master plan from the 1970 feasibility study for Telluride.** (*MacAllister.*)

6.3 *(Left)* **A ski ranch sensitively sited at the meeting of woodland and meadow.**

6.4 *(Right)* **The three terraces of condominiums were the only structures designed by the original design team.**

original investment the town had set about establishing a role for itself in this new leisure development. New businesses, such as catering, accommodation and specialist shopping sprang up. In order to keep these active during the summer period, festivals of all kinds were established ranging from chamber music, jazz and blue grass to hang-gliding and hot air ballooning. The old Opera House has been restored and extended and now hosts conferences and festivals. The town had built on the new winter developments to establish itself as a healthy concern. In order to maintain the skiing quality, however, it was now important to boost the mountain facilities. This required another permit from the Forest Service.

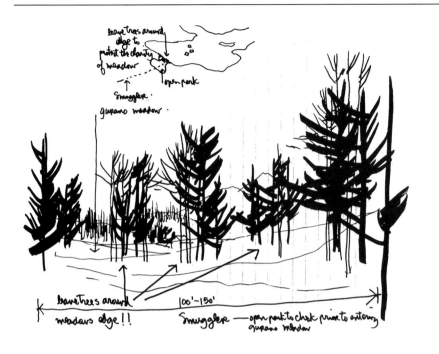

6.5 *(Left)* **A sketch by the landscape architect illustrating the hierarchy of spaces he wished the skier to experience, skiing from the spruce habitat into the meadows. (*Lovinger.*)**

6.6 *(Right)* **A sketch by the landscape architect showing the character aimed for on the main ski runs. The width of the run was to be narrow enough to give protection from snow-melt, and wide enough for ski races. A natural, feathered edge to the woodland was sought. (*Lovinger.*)**

THE NEW MASTER PLAN OF 1979

The resulting 1979 Master Plan was prepared largely in-house by the Telluride Ski Resort Company (Fig. 6.7). The aims were twofold: to increase the amount and quality of skiing; and to provide a base – the Mountain Village – to service year-round leisure activities. In order to finance these developments it became necessary to increase the amount of real estate in the project. To encourage prospective buyers, a golf course was prepared – as there are 45 million golfers as opposed to 6 million skiers in the US, the course would obviously widen the prospective market for home buyers.

This master plan also involved adjacent landowners and developers, and the Town and County. Through this involvement equitable methods of sharing costs for common services were established. As the prospective customers of the other developers would partly be attracted by the ski and golf facilities provided by Allred, it seemed only fair that they should contribute towards infrastructure costs.

The main differences in the 1979 master plan from the original are the southern shift of the entrance road and the base (renamed the Mountain Village); the proposed 18-hole

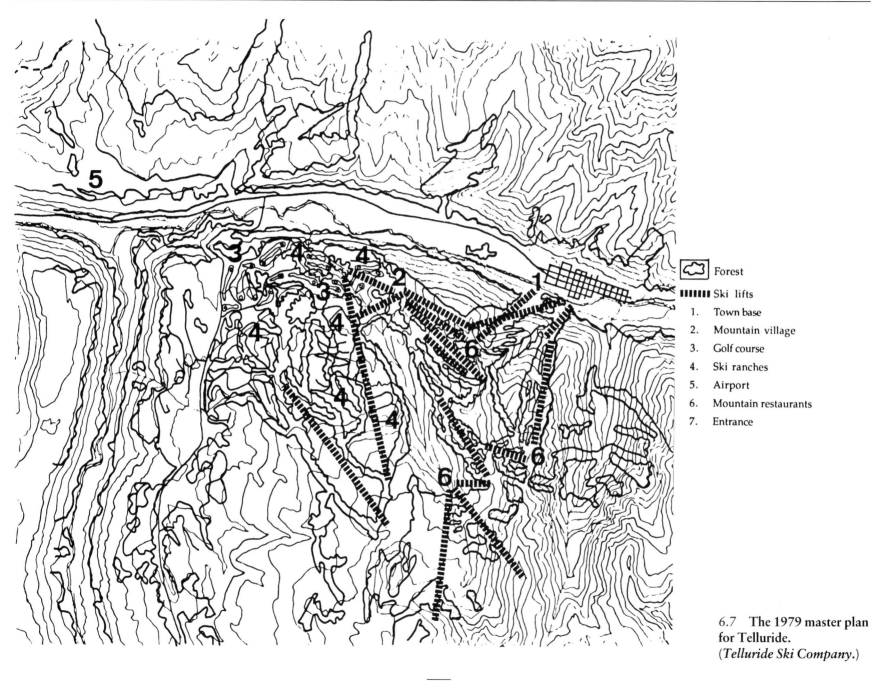

Forest

Ski lifts

1. Town base
2. Mountain village
3. Golf course
4. Ski ranches
5. Airport
6. Mountain restaurants
7. Entrance

6.7 **The 1979 master plan for Telluride.**
(*Telluride Ski Company.*)

6.8 *(Left)* **The buildings of the Mountain Village (left of centre) sit above the golf course and below the main ski runs. Early signs of real estate development can be seen (right of centre). Similar houses will fringe the entire golf course. The importance of the Ridgeline in unifying the site development is well illustrated.**

6.9 *(Right)* **The Mountain Village under construction. The ski runs directly behind the village are much wider and open – no islands of trees – than the landscape architect recommended. The new runs from Bald Mountains (right) are extremely crude, with no attempt made to feather the edges.**

golf course; the expansion of housing eastwards to the line of Prospect Creek, both in the woods and on the meadows around the golf course; a high-speed gondola to connect the Town Terminus and the Mountain Village; six new lifts and trails; four restaurants on the ski slopes; snow-making facilities; and the widening of the existing runs. The original master plan illustrated the Mountain Village as a compact facility, integrating service and commercial facilities with accommodation in one structure. It was also firmly located at the base of the ski area, acting as both beginning and end of the experience. In fact the Village now has a looser layout of individual buildings arranged around squares, and is located further up the slope. This siting allows the golf to begin and end at the Village, with the Club House and Hotel attached to the centre. The eighteenth fairway also provides a winter ski run from the Village to the base, either to pick up an express lift to the intermediate skiing area or the last run of the day home to the proposed golf-course housing (Fig. 6.8).

The style of development suggested in the proposals is in brick-built pitch-roofed vernacular – Colorado cuckoo clock, perhaps. The density and mass of development appears, from the model and sketches, to be rather overpowering for the site and too suburban in character. As yet too little has been built to be able to reach a proper judgement (Fig. 6.9). The increased level of individual house lots intruding into Prospect Meadow seems to be a gross overdevelopment of the site. The access roads are being carefully constructed, all bare embankments mulched and reseeded to control erosion and tree removal minimized. However, given the very steep landform and the size of house plots, when totally

6.10 (*Left*) **At present these ski-in, ski-out lodges sit well in their woodland environment. However, they are only the beginning of much more development throughout these steep, wooded areas. Further loss of tree cover can only add to the erosion of visual, soil and habitat quality.**

6.11 (*Right*) **Telluride ski area from the Ridgeline, which sweeps across the middle ground. Midway restaurant is in the foreground; Mountain Village right of middle ground; the golf course runs in front of the ridge. The new airport is on the central flat area across the valley.**

developed a once wooded landscape will undoubtedly be dominated by roofs and roads (Fig. 6.10). The 1972 master plan retained these areas for ski runs, partly for visual reasons but mainly because of the likelihood of erosion arising from such residential development.

In the broader landscape the effect of widening the ski runs is already apparent (Fig. 6.11). In place of the sensitively feathered edges, islands of trees and braided trails through the forest created by Lovinger, there are now sharp-edged runs of uniform width, crudely carving a way across the

mountainsides. As with the access roads, careful attention has been paid to erosion control measures. All runs have been reseeded, and on problem areas plastic netting and mulches have been used to bind the surface and speed plant growth (Fig. 6.12.) Lovinger set out in 1972 to design a total landscape experience for the skier, where one could appreciate the changing views, landforms and habitats, descending the ridge through spruce and aspen to the wide, bowl-like meadows. Today the runs seem merely functional, routes to carry ski traffic efficiently from the top of the mountain to the

bottom. Sadly, something of the Telluride mountain experience has been lost.

Wider concerns regarding the impact of the development on the natural systems and the local culture have been articulated by the conservationist Edward Abbey in an article entitled 'Telluride Blues – a hatchet job'. The tenor of his criticism is clear from the following quotation.

In 1970 a foreigner from California named Joseph T. Zoline moved in with $5 million and began the Californication of Telluride. Formerly an honest, decayed little mining town of about 300 souls, it is

6.12 **The Ridgeline ski run in summer.**
In contrast to the original design sketches, the run is uniform in width and treatment of the edges.

now a bustling whore of a ski resort with a population of 1,500 and many more to come. If all goes badly, as planned.[6]

While much of his objection is simply a rejection of change in any form to an area for which he feels a particular, personal empathy, he makes at least two valid criticisms that apply equally to such developments worldwide. Firstly, the existing local population gain little, if anything, from the development. Secondly, the scale, style and construction of the buildings are out of keeping with the local environment.

Developments of such a scale are largely dependent on outside finance, either private or governmental. Local people, usually a declining, ageing community with rural-based skills, lack the expertise and numbers to manage such projects. So outsiders are necessarily brought in to construct, establish and manage the scheme, leaving the locals to pick up unskilled jobs at each stage. It calls for extremely sensitive manipulation to ensure the integration and co-operation of locals and incomers as the development progresses.

New buildings are springing up in and around Telluride (Fig. 6.13). On the whole, the historic central core is well protected under the National Historic Landmark controls. Zoning codes clearly delimit landuses, and within these developers are encouraged to base their designs on local precedent. Thus brick and framed buildings are considered appropriate for the commercial areas, flat-roofed warehouse forms in the old manufacturing area (even when these forms disguise the inevitable condominiums) and timber cladding for residential buildings. On the mountain the Village and the housing built so far seems to

6.13 **Ski lift and runs at Telluride. The houses in the foreground are all new, a direct spin-off from the ski development.**

be in a watered-down post-modern style. But it is perhaps unfair to criticize something so incomplete. Abbey, however, is not impressed with the result so far, likening it to a haphazard arrangement of apple boxes. Other critics have referred to it as in the Disneyland mode – cute, vernacular, wood-and-shingle style. There are some who see it differently: 'Telluride' said a writer in *Ski Magazine*, 'is quite unlike any place you've ever seen before . . . an uncommon place which offers in abundance what other resorts can only dream of: antiquity, style, distinction, infinite, unadulterated beauty.'[7] This assessment would seem to show that the client market sought by the Telluride developers is well satisfied. There are some indications, however, which suggest that Telluride is merely at the beginning of change. The most recent master plan for the region, in July 1989, forecasts a population ceiling in the region of 17–22,000. This will be accommodated partly on the Mountain, but also within the town boundary and alongside the river, in a western expansion of clustered development.

When this expansion occurs it is vital that the present visual separation between the town of Telluride and the complementary valley of the San Miguel river, and the Mountain Village and the ski developments is rigorously maintained. At present this sharply-defined contrast between the gridded, regular town and the freer, flowing development pattern allows each to develop a very individual and strong relationship with the landscape. The town is almost stamped upon the land, like a rancher's brand on a steer, while the ski development attempts to relate to both the landform and the vegetation. The wooded northern slope of the ridge thus acts as both connector and divider, allowing each to display its own personality.

Both master plans (1970 and 1979) defined the importance of developing these twin poles as linked but individual elements to enrich the overall character of the final project. At the moment this still seems to be happening, but the developers must continue to be vigilant in protecting the integrity of the ridge line. Otherwise the unique landscape and townscape qualities of the area will be diluted, and the development will degenerate into another piece of suburban subtopia.

7

Conclusions and a final case study
Canberra

The five case studies have shown something of the depth and diversity of skills and knowledge that a landscape architect brings to bear during the design and implementation of a project. They have shown that although there may not be a common approach to organizing and manipulating the many inputs necessary to achieve a reasonable solution to a design problem, they all follow rational, logical and verifiable methods. This process has been shown in action in projects ranging in scale from interpreting and classifying a river system through the regeneration of urban areas to the level of single-function projects. At all levels the designers have juggled with the major elements informing the process of designing: the brief, the concept and technical knowledge. Solutions to problems set by the brief have been tested against constraints – or opportunities – perceived through sifting site information. Conversely ideas springing from an appreciation and comprehension of inherent site qualities have been rigorously tested

against client and user needs. The feasibility of concepts is similarly evaluated to judge their appropriateness, durability and economy.

The case studies have also been looked at over time, to describe and evaluate how the original design, documented and supervised by the landscape architect, has since progressed. Change must occur, but it has not always been in the form envisaged by the designer. Sometimes this has been due to reasons one could not reasonably be expected to foresee. For example in the Diplomatic Quarter in Ar-riyadh, the decision by the government not to proceed with the housing element occurred after the major infrastructure was installed and planting completed. This has had two obvious effects: the visual gaps in the urban pattern and the continuing calls on potable water for irrigation instead of treated effluent from the expected residents.

Change may be anticipated by the designer but the techniques and programming to

respond to it may not be clearly communicated to the long-term managers of the project. At Stirling University, for example, the overall structure of the new campus landscape has been strong enough to accept buildings of a character and function not anticipated by the master planning; yet the bold, simple shapes, forms and colours of the planting design are being undermined by a management policy that shows little understanding of the original design philosophy. The need to overcome similar problems arising from a breakdown between design and management expectations led to the follow-on contracts developed by the SDA in Glasgow. These were the two-year establishment periods for each contract, funded by the SDA rather than the owners of the finished projects, the Glasgow Parks Department. Monitoring of these establishment contracts resulted in a management manual, a document providing the Parks Department with detailed information regarding design and maintenance objectives, a description of how these have actually been met over a two-year-period and a cost breakdown, in terms of labour and mechanical input, over this same period. This has enabled the Parks authority to anticipate and budget realistically for the extra costs or changes in procedures required in managing these new areas of open space.

The landscape architect has also been shown in the role of an enabler, both in making people aware of previously disregarded resources, such as the Parramatta River, and in using landscape projects to teach skills and generate employment, as at Barrowfield in Glasgow. The Parramatta Study has been used by municipalities and amenity groups as a stimulus to ensure that changes on or adjacent to the river contribute to the rehabilitation of it as a total system. It provides a baseline of data and a set of values against which development projects may be judged. The original team who prepared the document has played little part in implementing the physical and biotic changes since 1976. However, their study provides a framework within which many others have worked, gradually creating a new, more useful and more widely appreciated environment for working, living and leisure.

In contrast the landscape architect at Barrowfield has been a key member of the various groups and organizations that are improving the work opportunities and the living environment for the residents. Here it is the actual implementation and continuing management of projects on the ground that provide the basis for the physical, social and economic regeneration of this particular community.

CANBERRA – THE SITE

To draw these strands of the design process together it is useful to study one more project, one that has been evolving over some 80 years. This is the City of Canberra, the administrative capital of Australia. The site was selected by a surveyor, largely on the basis of water catchment; the master plan was conceived by an American architect and landscape designer, Walter Burley Griffin; the bones of his layout were set down, fleshed out and nurtured by a forester, Thomas Weston; and after 50 years of faltering commitment the project was carried forward by an interdisciplinary authority, the National Capital Development Corporation (NCDC). Canberra is generally recognized as a city that owes its pleasant character to the way in which is has been related to the pre-existing landscape and the manner in which it has created lakes and established trees on a bleak, open plain.

It is hard to imagine Canberra without trees, and without lakes but if it were, the City would be quite undistinguished. Its architecture, general built form or layout is insufficient to bind the urban area, to create a unity from disparate components.[1]

Surveyor Scrivener examined many sites in the course of his task to find a suitable setting for the national capital of the recently federated States of the Commonwealth of Australia. His effective client, the Minister of Home Affairs, directed that 'the federal Capital should be a beautiful city, occupying a commanding position with extensive views and embracing distinctive features, which will lend themselves to a design worthy of the object, not only for the present, but for all time.'[2]

The site chosen in 1908 certainly included these features of the brief, providing a landscape setting with distinctly Australian characteristics (Fig. 7.1). To meet his remit of ensuring an adequate water catchment for the new settlement. Scrivener's boundary to the new Australian Capital Territory embraced the surrounding hills – including the impressive Brindabella Range – and some 50km (30 miles) of the Murrumbidgee River, a part of the extensive Murray River system. There had been European settlement in the area since 1824, with large grazing farms in the plains and smaller holdings on the surrounding hills. These smaller units had cleared much of the vegetation resulting in erosion. The higher and steeper hills, however, were still thickly wooded.

This foresight on the part of the Federal Government in acquiring so much land has had many subsequent benefits for the citizens of Canberra, not least in providing an area of native bush very accessible to the city.

However, the original legislators were more concerned about the possibility of political blackmail from the surrounding State Government of New South Wales if it controlled the water supply to the capital.

The acquisition by the government of freehold land and its adoption of a leasehold system of land tenure have been used as planning tools in organizing orderly and economic control of land-use systems and urban development. It also enabled Weston to implement his far-reaching structure and forestry planting in advance of any buildings. The actual site for the city was in the north of the Australian Capital Territory (ACT), in the valley of the Molonglo River, a tributary of the Murrumbidgee. This was in the form of an open, rolling grass plain at some 550m (1800ft) elevation, enclosed by a circle of bare hills rising to over 810m (2658ft). The Molonglo cut its way through this bowl, flowing from east to west. Willows (*Salix sp.*) introduced by the settlers, lined the river, and other exotics such as *Ulmus sp.* marked the scattered farms and the church. The area receives an annual average of 580mm (23 in.) rainfall, experiences cool winters, with a mean low temperature of 1°C, and cold winter winds from the north-west sector. Summers are dry with a mean maximum of 28°C. The soils are relatively poor, with a high clay content.

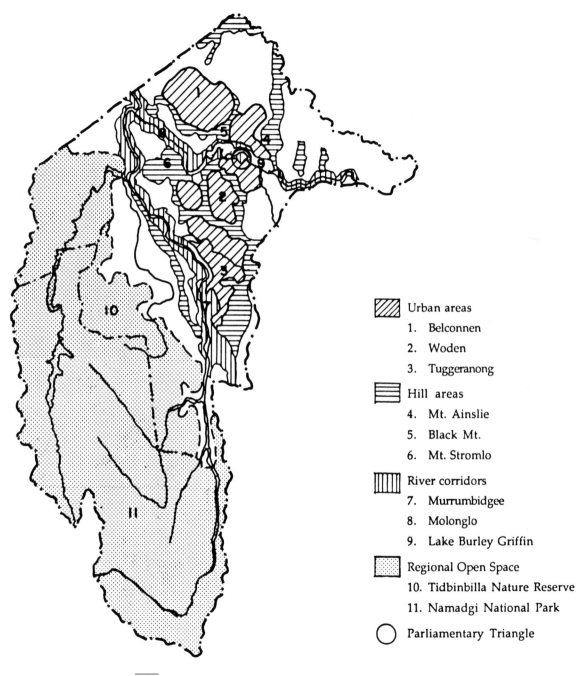

Urban areas
1. Belconnen
2. Woden
3. Tuggeranong

Hill areas
4. Mt. Ainslie
5. Black Mt.
6. Mt. Stromlo

River corridors
7. Murrumbidgee
8. Molonglo
9. Lake Burley Griffin

Regional Open Space
10. Tidbinbilla Nature Reserve
11. Namadgi National Park

Parliamentary Triangle

7.1 **Canberra open space system.** (*NCDC.*)

GRIFFIN'S SCHEME

Griffin's prize-winning scheme of 1912 for the new capital is the image most people have of Canberra, particularly through the beautifully rendered drawings by his wife Marion Mahoney. In reality, however, only one building designed by Griffin was constructed by the time his contract as Federal Director of Design and Construction was terminated in 1920. During his seven years in Canberra he worked closely with the afforestation and horticultural officer, Weston. The planting during this time, and up until Weston's retirement in 1926, set a landscape structure and pattern that guided subsequent development. Griffin's concept has been separately described as following the style of both the American City Beautiful movement and the English Garden City. In a sense his design does combine elements from both. The wide boulevards and vistas with an emphasis on imposing built-form to control geometry are analogous with heroic City Beautiful patterns, while his understanding and manipulation of the existing topography and natural vistas and the tree-lined residential layouts resemble Garden City concepts. The Emersonian social principles that underpinned the design were one element that has subsequently been almost totally diluted.[3]

Griffin's design was three dimensional. By its geometry and heroic scale it created a relationship on the ground between the valleys and the hills and determined that buildings would forever be subordinated to the landscape. The sites for buildings of substance in the Capital were chosen by Griffin to be on the valley floor and thus not to compete with the hills, even small hills in the basin. He proposed a canopy of trees under which the residential area would lie. Public buildings were permitted to rise above the canopy or relate to each other across plazas which were not to be adorned or confused by trees. . . . In Griffin's words, the marriage of built and natural forms would secure 'a horizontal distribution of the large masses for more and better air, sunlight, verdure and beauty.'[4]

So although he supervised none of the built components within his plan, through Weston's planting much of his tree canopy was established. The plan located the city in the bowl of hills on both sides of a series of lakes formed by damming the Molonglo. These lakes formed the water axes, the base of his Parliamentary Triangle containing the seat of government and administration. From the apex of this triangle – Capitol Hill – he carried a land axis northwards at right angles to the lake axis to focus on Mount Ainslie. Shorter vistas along the sides of the triangle focused on smaller hills over the lake.

Largely due to the outbreak of war in 1914, no construction work went ahead on the new Capital until Griffin's dismissal in 1920. The slightly amended plan, however, was gazetted by the Commonwealth Parliament, and was the basis for subsequent work. It was also the layout that directed the planting schemes of Weston. On his appointment, Weston set himself four objectves: to establish a nursery, to raise and test nursery stock deemed suitable for the Canberra area, to re-afforest the enclosing hills; and to procure from as many sources as possibly commercial and ornamental seeds, for propagation and testing, for their adaptability to Canberra.

These still seem sensible objectives, given the character of the site he had to deal with. No other Australian city had been established at such an elevation. Much of the existing vegetation had been removed, and the soils depleted by compaction and overgrazing. There was no precedent for the task of establishing planting in such an area at such an altitude and for such a purpose. His success can be seen in the nursery he began, which still operates; his experimental arboretum now leased as a golf course; the central parks such as Haig, City Hill and Telopea; the early residential area of Reid; the re-vegetation of the enclosing hills; and his commercial reafforestation on Mount Stromlo. Weston also planted the main vista from the Parliamentary Triangle and established structure planting within this area itself (Fig. 7.2).

Progress on the City languished after Weston's retirement, due firstly to the depression and then the Second World War. In 1944, however, Lindsay Pryor, a botanist, was appointed as first Director of the Parks Section of the Department of the Capital Territory, the government agency responsible for administering the ACT. Pryor continued and extended Weston's experiments with plant species, both native and exotic, and was also responsible for establishing a National Botanic Garden. This is at the foot of Black Mountain and concentrates on native Australian flora.

7.2 **Formal street planting by Weston.**

THE NATIONAL CAPITAL DEVELOPMENT CORPORATION

In 1958 the Commonwealth Government set up a National Capital Development Corporation (NCDC) to plan and supervise the development of the city. This followed a long period of stagnation or slow, fragmented growth since the gazetting of Griffin's plan in 1925. But the expansion of Canberra, often referred to as a 'bush' capital, was now underway, mainly as a result of a more buoyant Australian economy, and a period of political stability. The government had appointed Sir William Holford, a London-based architect, planner and landscape architect, to advise on how best to approach the expansion of the city. It was his suggestion to set up a multi-disciplinary design organization like the NCDC.

Holford also reappraised the Griffin plan

against the demands of the mid 1950s. With a population of some 50,000, the city had already exceeded the numbers the Griffin plan was designed for. It was obvious that growth in population would continue as government departments shifted their bases to Canberra. These public servants would also require services, both private sector, such as retail and entertainment, and public, such as health centres, schools and leisure facilities. Since 1909 the private motor car had also become a major fact of life, making demands on urban space.

Holford reported that the central core of Griffin's design should remain to guide development within the city centre. However, the arterial road system would need expanding to carry and distribute the present and estimated numbers of private vehicles. He suggested that, in line with Garden City principles, there should be no expansion of the Griffin plan. Rather the topographical edge should be reinforced with planting, and new, satellite settlements should be planned beyond this greenbelt, in similarly discrete landscape units. These would have a population of around 50,000, and be similar in concept to the British new towns of the period. Within the core area Holford suggested that high priority should be given to establishing the central lake, according to Griffin's plan for a water axis, which would visually draw the physically separated Parliamentary and Civic areas together. He produced design proposals for this that were accepted and were among the first major tasks carried out by the NCDC.

Since 1958, the population of Canberra has grown to some 260,000 people. This growth is expected to continue, but at a reduced rate. To meet this increase, and to ensure an agreeable lifestyle for the citizens, the NCDC have produced and implemented projects at planning level and at detailed project design level. They have implemented two new towns, a third is under construction and a fourth is at final planning stage. They have also been involved in rationalizing the development of the central business centre and the Parliamentary triangle. Landscape architects have continued to play a major part in these developments. Within NCDC the landscape team are involved at all stages of development, from broad-scale planning to implementation. In addition they have moved outside the municipal area and put forward proposals for a 'national capital open space system' to analyse the wider areas of the ACT and classify the variety and level of recreational uses. These range from National Park areas in the Brindabellas, through use of the water catchment at Cotter Dam and along the Murrumbidgee, to an inner greenbelt or ridge system to ensure a rational use of this necessary visual barrier (see Fig. 7.1).

Management of all open spaces is undertaken by the Department of National Capital Territories (NCT). The Parks Section controls the municipal areas while the National Parks and Conservation Section has responsibility for the rural land. Large parts of the ACT are still farmed under short-term lease; some are on land being held for future urban expansion, but other areas will continue as open space for the forseeable future. The NCT Conservation Section is at present reviewing these to see if the farmers can be given much longer leases to encourage them to manage the land better. At present they are understandably reluctant to invest in long-term projects, such as tree planting, when their tenure is insecure.

The National Parks and Wildlife Section also manage heritage sites, such as the Lanyon Estate. This is currently being rehabilitated to illustrate the various stages and effects on the landscape of agricultural developments which have occurred in the 150-odd years since European settlement (Fig. 7.3). Within the city there are many organizations and institutions – hospitals, tertiary education, commercial and industrial concerns – that also involve development. Through the leasehold system unique in Australia to the ACT, the NCDC can control the location, design and management of these. Leasees not meeting the requirements of their lease can have these withdrawn.

This tenure system has enabled the landscape development 'to proceed on a comprehensive basis'.[5] To demonstrate this point, the five following aspects or projects are discussed in more detail: a comparison between the open space system in Belconnen and Tuggeranong new towns; the evolution of Commonwealth Park over some 20 years; the current urban design proposals for the Parliamentary Triangle; a comparison of the campus plans for the Australian National University and the Canberra College of Advanced Education; and the design and management proposals for the Fern Hill Technology Park.

7.3 An avenue of *Pinus radiata* leads to the National Trust property of Lanyon. This nineteenth-century homestead is carefuly managed to retain historic and cultural values.

OPEN SPACES IN
BELCONNEN AND TUGGERANONG

The NCDC have published their guidelines for urban open space standards, design and management.[6] The standards are based on an empirical review of those used by other authorities, adjusted to meet the conditions prevailing at Canberra. They specify three main items: the amount of open space to be allocated for every 1000 persons; the ratio of each of five separate types of open space classified within the overall total; and development and maintenance standards for each type of project. Although five types of open space are described, these are not planned or designed as discrete units. More often they are combined into larger, multi-purpose parcels of land. This not only

140

generates more use of the areas, but it can also decrease maintenance and management costs. In the earlier new town, Belconnen, the standards were applied very much as prescribed, giving an even pattern and grain to the neighbourhoods. The generally rolling topography had no immediately recognizable landmarks, and the consequent balance of open space and built form is rather bland and monotonous (Fig. 7.4). It is difficult for a stranger to distinguish one suburban neighbourhood from another. The open space units, whilst large within themselves, merge imperceptibly into the adjacent housing areas without any clear edge or spatial definition. There is no strong sense of place or individual character, except in small pockets where localized contrasts in topography occur, such as at Aranda.

Similarly the town centre at present has a poor relationship with the town park and Lake Ginninderra. The buildings have been pulled back from the water's edge and have no visual or physical connection with each other. This is being rectified in a few cases, for instance a Further Education College and some small businesses and cafés are now sited next to the lake. However, the general character of this town park is still essentially rural and seems peripheral to the functioning of the town centre.

By contrast in Tuggeranong, the town centre development approaches the lake frontage, and medium-density housing has been introduced into a parkland setting next to the water. As in Belconnen, the lake will also function as an important recreational area, with a town park, three beach and barbecue areas, and a system of footpaths and cycleways. The northern end, as at Lake Ginninderra, is being protected as a bird refuge, whilst sailing and board-sailing are

7.4   Belconnen Street. The typical Canberra 'nature strip' fronts all suburban developments, achieving a pleasantly informal street unity. Householders can claim free trees and shrubs from the NCDC plant nursery.

encouraged on the central and southern areas. Both lakes have an important role in protecting the water quality of the Murrumbidgee River, by controlling urban run-off and containing silt and pollutants; each includes a series of upstream settling ponds.

The general distribution of open space in Tuggeranong is quite different to that at Belconnen. Largely as a result of the more pronounced topography, most of the playing fields and parks have been combined in the flatter land, giving a more unified and extended character to the whole, such as in

Kambah district. Also due to the topography, housing developments were here concentrated into sectors, with a population three to four times larger than in Belconnen's neighbourhoods. These surround, and focus on, their large blocks of recreational open space and are contained by the prominent surrounding hills such as Mount Taylor and Mount Neighbour. There is thus a strong contrast between the urban form and the land form as well as a definition to the urban edge. Primary and secondary schools and community buildings are closely integrated with the parkland. Playing fields are grouped

in larger blocks, serving both schools and the general public. This leads to savings in maintenance and management, and service facilities can also be shared.

Larger unified areas of open space, as at Kambah, are generally more efficient in terms of management. Personnel can operate from one depot, machinery can be larger and hence complete operations more rapidly and general economies of scale can keep down annual maintenance budgets. In Kambah the close integration of educational and recreational facilities has also led to the provision of large, well-supervised play parks. These provide a

7.5   The sectorial open space of Kambah carefully relates play areas to schools and housing.

7.6 The pedestrian path winds through the linear open space of Kambah, linking the town centre to schools, housing and sports facilities.

series of challenging and well-designed structures, for climbing, swinging, BMX cycling and skate boarding (Fig. 7.5). At a less energetic level footpaths and cycleways cross the parkland, connecting the housing and shopping areas to each other and the various educational, community and recreational facilities (Fig. 7.6). Where roads cross the open space wide underpasses allow the open space to safely flow under these obstructions.

In summary, both Belconnen and Tuggeranong have followed the NCDC planning provisions for open space. Largely as a result of different topography, however, the form and distribution of public parks, playing fields and play facilities is completely different in each township. In Tuggeranong it is aggregated into large, continuous units serving sectorial needs. Belconnen, in contrast, has focused the open space provisions at the smaller neighbourhood level, giving a more even visual balance between the built and unbuilt environments.

COMMONWEALTH PARK

Commonwealth Park, one of a series of parks ringing the shore of Lake Burley Griffin, is a good example of how a landscape design can grow in complexity over time. The key to success is a good basic master plan to establish a strong structure and character, and a continuing design involvement with the management team responsible for day-to-day care and maintenance. With the exception of a few unfortunate elements, the master plan for Commonwealth Park has been robust enough to respond to changing pressures over the 25 years of its existence (Fig. 7.7).

The master plan was prepared by Dame Sylvia Crowe, the distinguished British landscape architect, in the early 1960s. Since then the elements of her proposals have been gradually implemented, until in the late 1980s the project is all but complete. This element of phasing is an important factor in most landscape designs. Work is often not completed under one contract, sometimes not even for one client or by the same designer. The master plan, or management plan, must take this fact into account, and ensure that the partly implemented project appears as a finite whole at each phase. The structuring of the site, by a combination of circulation routes, ground modelling and planting, is the best way to achieve this sense of unity. Later, more detailed additions can be absorbed sympathetically within this initial landscape framework.

At Commonwealth Park, the master plan established a series of major and minor spaces, and suggested a range of functions or character for each setting. The focus of the design was the Nerang Pool, a body of water set back from the shoreline of Lake Burley Griffin and generally screened from the larger water area by landform and planting. Similarly an earth mound and heavy planting screened out the four-lane Parkes Way and minimized the impact of the office blocks beyond. Eastwards along the lake shore an open eucalyptus woodland led to the grand axis of Anzac Parade, visually connecting the War Memorial and Mount Ainslie with the Parliamentary Triangle and Red Hill. On the west the rolling land between the lake and

Commonwealth Avenue was structured into a series of spaces to provide an outdoor theatre, conservatories, car parking and a restaurant. The ground here falls more steeply to Lake Burley Griffin, and the restaurant was to take advantage of the views this offered across the lake to the national buildings on the southern shore. The Crowe master plan, therefore, envisaged a broad parkland, with the more complex elements placed around the nodal Nerang Pool.

This central area was seen as a series of theme gardens, each displaying an individual character but linked by the common element of water. Themes such as a stream valley,

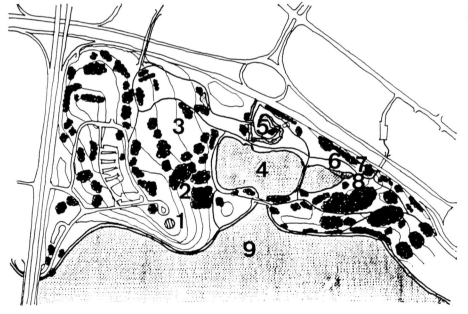

1. Regatta Point
2. Rhododendron garden
3. Outdoor theatre
4. Nerang pool
5. Marsh gardens
6. Play fort
7. Amphitheatre
8. Stream valley
9. Lake Burley Griffin

marsh gardens and lily ponds were suggested (Fig. 7.8). During the 1960s these concepts around the pond were developed and implemented by landscape architects within the NCDC, particularly Richard Clough and Margaret Hendry. Their realization of these ideas has generally been successful.

During the 1970s and 1980s the park continued to develop in detail. In the western area the structure planting was reinforced, a rhododendron garden completed and a new pool with associated sculpture constructed. A permanent exhibition of NCDC planning combined with a restaurant was designed in an attractive pavilion on Regatta Point. To supplement the extremely popular children's water play area, a stone fort playground was built. One unfortunate addition has been the construction of a permanent building for outdoor theatrical performances. The siting of this and the ground-modelling around it are rather crude, and it is probable that the spectator area will need to be fenced off to enable entrance charges to be made. One of the important spaces linking the parkland to the pond will thereby be removed from general public use.

Otherwise, the sequence of spaces through the park – from the broader, simpler parkland through the more enclosed rhododendron garden into the intimate marsh and water gardens and back to the wide spaces next to the pool – gives a variety of scales and a diversity of use and interest that is extremely satisfying and appealing. This is reinforced when the expansive views over the lake are opened out, either at water level on the eastern promenade, or from the heights of Regatta Point.

The park has remained true to the spirit of the original master plan. This is in part a reflection of the quality of that plan, and of

7.7 (Left) **Commonweath Park. (NCDC).**

7.8 (Right) **The Marsh Garden.**

the subsequent detailed design contracts through which it was realized. It is also a result of the continuing interest and involvement of the NCDC landscape architects. Although the park is now managed by the Parks Section of the Department of National Capital Territories, the NCDC are still consulted about proposed changes arising from maintenance or management needs. This continuing liaison between designer and manager is essential if the original spirit of the design is to be retained. In this case the master plan concept seems robust enough to respond to changing demands, but these changes must nonetheless respect the qualities and values inherent in the designs.

THE PARLIAMENTARY ZONE

On a larger scale the Parliamentary Zone is an interesting example of how successive designers over the years have variously interpreted the original Griffin plan.

In 1986 the NCDC published a development plan for the Parliamentary Zone, the triangle of land with Parliament House at the apex, the southern lakeshore as its base and Commonwealth and Kings Avenues as its sides (Fig. 7.9). This plan recognized the uncoordinated appearance of this important area, a reflection of the changing political and planning moods in Canberra since the original Griffin plan. At present only some 5 per cent of the land surface is built on, whilst twice this amount is devoted to visually intrusive surface car parking. The present building locations vary in architectural style, and their locations were often determined by now superseded master plans. The High Court, for example, was sited to relate to a proposed lakeside Parliament House, connected by decks and walkways over underground car parks.

It was an incomplete development and presented a somewhat forlorn appearance. It was as if the Hydro from some Edwardian Spa had been transported to the municipal park of a country town and surrounded by car parks in which floated three enormous-scale edifices from an architectural age best forgotten.[7]

Griffin's prize-winning scheme of 1912 had shown a Capitol building as the southern climax of his land axis. He located Parliament House north on the lower Camp Hill, to illustrate the subservience of the legislators to the nation. Thus the Capitol building – a place of popular assembly, a temple to the national spirit and a focus for the Australian national consciousness – would express the democratic principles inherent in the constitution, and so visually dominate the seat of parliament.[8] As Griffin never clearly articulated the role or form of this democratic temple, it was never fully accepted by successive governments and planners. Or perhaps it was deliberately misunderstood, as the power of the legislators grew. Although the Provisional Parliament House (opened in 1927) was placed so as not to compromise either the Camp Hill or Capitol Hill locations, it was not until 1974 that Capitol Hill was finally agreed upon as the site for the new Parliament House. In 1980 a plan for the zone proposed a selective reinstatement of Griffin's original principles. This plan established the guidelines for the New Parliament House design competition. The winning scheme, now completed, is centred on the land axis, which largely generates the plan form of the building. Griffin's overriding symbol of the democratic nature of constitutional Government has been cleverly subsumed within the design articulated by the flag mast that rises some 80m (260ft) above the seemingly grass-roofed building. The Australian public appears to appreciate the building, as it was visited by over 1 million people in its first year of operation, a figure not expected to be reached until after five years.

The 1986 NCDC plan was a response to the awareness that these visitors, and the increasing numbers of public servants working in the area, would expect a better environment in the Parliamentary Zone, together with services and transport. It established four basic principles: to complete the Griffin Land Axis; to identify future

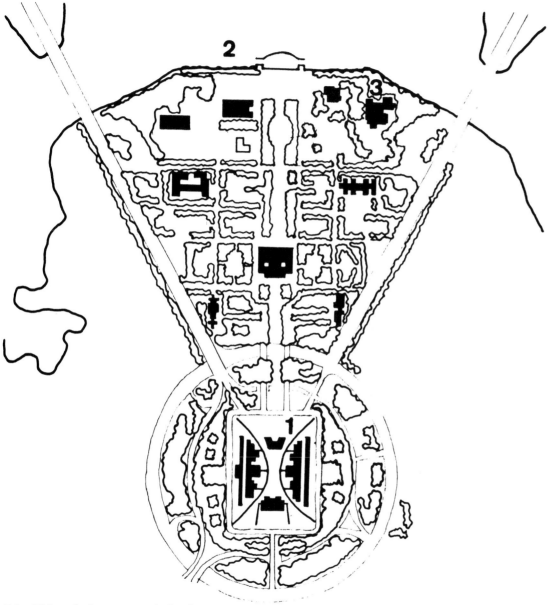

7.9 Urban design proposals for the Parliamentary Triangle. 1 New Parliament House; 2 Lake Burley Griffin; 3 National Gallery.

building sites; to progressively improve the landscape quality; and to improve transport, parking and consumer facilities.

Whilst open space covers over 70 per cent of the Triangle, the treatment of this also varies, from highly manicured formal gardens, through exotic avenues of trees, to native planting. Early tree planting by Weston articulated the form of Griffin's plan, but more recent schemes have been freer in character.

The quality of landscape in the Parliamentary Zone is very patchy, yet critical for both environmental and visual reasons. The Zone generally, by virtue of its northwards orientation, is largely exposed to adverse climates in terms of summer sun and prevailing winter winds, thus from the point of view of pedestrians, tree and shrub plantings are the most effective and economical means of sheltering outdoor spaces and pathways.[9]

The 1986 development plan proposes a basic pattern of roads and land subdivisions, identifies possible building sites and indicates in general terms how a new landscape structure will delineate roads and pathways and enclose gardens, recreation spaces and future building sites. It foresees trees acting as the major space makers in the Zone for a long time to come in the form of both lines or avenues and freer clusters. The plant material will be predominantly native 'with the selective use of exotic species for heightened interest and seasonal colour.'[10]

In essence the plan is structured around a central spine, or mall, which will strengthen and complete Griffin's land axis. The proportions of the mall are based on those of

Anzac Parade, which continues the land axis across the lake. Dubbed Capitol Parade by the planners, it will consist of a dual carriageway separated by a wide median strip. This central space will be tree-lined, and subdivided into a series of smaller spaces for various active and passive uses. The carriageways will provide for both vehicular and pedestrian movement between Capitol Hill and the foreshore, across the land bridge designed and constructed as part of the New Parliament House project. Future buildings will face the Parade, and a major civic space is proposed in front of the Provisional Parliament House which will be refurbished as a major tourist information and interpretation centre.

At the lake shore, to signify the junction of the land and water axes, a formal terrace is proposed. The rear terrace wall extends east and west to embrace and unify the existing High Court building and the proposed Archive building. The terrace will incorporate a ferry and tourist bus interchange, a lake-shore promenade, a cycle path and a roadway. Formal avenues of exotic trees along the promenade will contrast with strong groups of trees balancing the High Court and National Library.

This plan is of particular interest as it demonstrates the need to establish a clear and workable set of overriding principles to guide long-term, and often unpredictable, development. It shows the need to explore thoroughly and define the spatial quality and character that the development should aim to achieve, drawing on the principles established by Griffin and adapting these to changed needs and values. But it also shows an awareness of the extended timescale over which development will occur. In recognizing this the 1986 plan illustrates the importance of bold tree, hedge and shrub planting both to define and articulate the major and minor spaces in advance of building mass and to create a more pleasant external environment.

This section on the Parliamentary Zone concludes by briefly describing two separate projects within the area – the New Parliament House and the sculpture garden of the Australian National Gallery.

Opened in 1988, to coincide with the Bicentenary of European settlement in Australia, it is obviously too soon to evaluate how the landscape elements of the Parliament building have evolved over time. What is of interest, however, is how the design team have rejected the obvious option to create a monumental building to dominate the Canberra townscape. Instead they have concealed what is in fact a massive building covering some 32ha (80 acres) under a reconstructed Capitol Hill, and clothed the flanks of this with plantations of eucalypts. As a result it is the flagpole, on its Calder-like stainless steel legs, which creates the city-wide skyline landmark. Individual building elements, such as the entrance loggia and the two legislative chambers are cleverly articulated to break the mass of the building down to a scale more compatible with suburban Canberra.

Although this design solution leads to a sympathetic match between building, landform and townscape, it required massive earthmoving and restructuring to achieve. Some 16m (52ft) of earth and rock were removed from the top of Capitol Hill and consequently all the existing native vegetation. Similarly Camp Hill was substantially lowered to form the land bridge over the road system and complete the Griffin land axis. These major changes to the natural landform and vegetation have been carried out extremely well, and so far the new landscape knits seamlessly into the old. At present the spaces forming the land axis are too open, but once the trees have become established, their rapid growth rate – up to 2m (6½ft) per annum – will soon provide the spatial effect envisaged by the designers (Fig. 7.10). Similarly the overpowering bulk of the east and west flanks will quickly be visually absorbed by the belts of fast-growing native trees.

The growth rate of native species is well illustrated by the sculpture garden, a 3 ha (7.5 acre) site on the north side of the Australian National Gallery. The garden was planted in 1980, on an area used for storage and working by the building contractor during construction of the Gallery. Consequently the soil was severely compacted and strewn with the usual post-contract rubble and rubbish. So prior to any planting, very careful ground preparation took place – ripping and harrowing, and the introduction of imported sandy soil and compost.

Planting was used in the design both to define spaces and to soften the strong, harsh natural light of Canberra. Four broad areas were created, each to reflect a different season. These also reflected the varying soil conditions, which ranged from shallow sandy soils to wet boggy areas. The ground surface is generally finished in gravel to allow free visitor movement among the trees without damage to grass or ground covers. The plant

species were mixed to create layers of vegetation at varying heights and were densely planted to encourage rapid, extended growth. Eucalyptus species planted at 500mm (19½in.) height were over 5m (16½ft) tall two years later. As a result of careful ground preparation and sensible species selection, this growth-rate has been sustained, and the sculpture garden today is extremely successful (Fig. 7.11). The spaces vary in scale and character to reflect the sculptures displayed, and the sequence of visual experiences is a stimulating interplay of art and nature.

7.10   **A fountain in the forecourt of the new Parliament Building.**

7.11   Native plant material has created the setting for the sculpture garden of the Australian National Gallery.

CAMPUS PLANS

Contrasting approaches to planting design, and to the siting and layout of the buildings, are very apparent in the campus plans for the Australian National University (ANU) and the Canberra College of Advanced Education (CCAE). Typically Griffin was not content merely to provide a site for the university. His plan of 1912 contained a campus plan based on a diagram justifying, on educational grounds, the choice of site and the spatial relationships between the 27 faculties. Black Mountain was not only to provide a topographical backcloth to the campus, it would also provide for botanical and silvicultural research, and opportunities for mineralogical and mining studies. Thus he located Natural Sciences, Agriculture and Mining next to the hill. With similar logic he placed Law and Commerce adjacent to the Civic Centre.

The Australian National University campus, although using the Griffin site and responding to his planning grids, is in fact an incoherent jumble of buildings.

Even within inner Canberra, several of the developed precincts rely heavily upon their landscaping for coherence and orientation. The Australian National University is a case in point. Functionally indecipherable to the stranger, the campus is a collection of unlike buildings, set among trees and linked after a fashion, by disconnected roads. Without the unifying canopy of trees, the University would look as undistinguished as its built form really is.[11]

In detail, some of the earlier planting is equally incoherent. However, over the last few years the ANU have been consciously attempting to use the planting, together with a rationalized circulation system, to improve the structure of the campus (Fig. 7.12). Entrances have been emphasized and the formal layout of the central core reinforced. To contrast with these geometric spaces, freer forms of open space are being created alongside Sullivan's Creek. This small body of water splits the campus in two physically. The recent landscape design, however, cleverly uses it visually to connect and unify the dispersed buildings on either bank. Exotic species have been planted in the central area of the campus and on the eastern boundary with central Canberra.

This core planting is complemented by peripheral planting of strong bands and groups of native species. These blend in with similar natural material on the lake shore and on the slopes of Black Mountain.

At the CCAE campus in Belconnen, native planting has been used throughout. It provides a useful demonstration of the fact that Australian plants can provide as much interest, in form, colour and texture, as exotics. The campus sits on the crest of a hill, with Lake Ginninderra and Belconnen town centre to the west and the Fern Hill Technology Park to the east. The teaching buildings run in two linked blocks along the ridge, giving largely east and west aspects to the rooms. Sportsfields are arranged on the east, while a line of student residences spill down the steeper slope towards Belconnen. Otherwise this western side is heavily planted with eucalyptus and casuarina.

Although more tightly organized and coherent in colour, scale and material, the CCAE buildings are extremely bland if not downright dull. It is the broad-scale planting

7.12 **Formal use of poplars on the Australian University campus.**

outside the built core that makes the strongest impression and gives a special character to these more extensive areas. The indigenous species have also encouraged native wildlife. Wallabies are a common sight in the woods, and there are numerous varieties of birds.

The enclosed spaces within the teaching spine carry on the theme of native planting. Tall white-trunked eucalypts provide a vertical element in the larger grassed courtyards. Varieties of acacia are used to structure the smaller, more intimate areas. Lower shrubs and ground-covers complement these and reinforce the spatial framework. These also provide detailed interest from leaf colour and texture, the form of their branches and stems and the seasonal colour of their flowers.

Recently there has been a reaction by Australian landscape architects against the use of native species in urban areas. One of their major objections has been the dullness of these plants, and the fact that, being evergreen, they do not reflect the changing seasons. The considered planting at CCAE would largely seem to refute this claim.

Another objection is the problem of managing such plant material in what is really an artificial environment for it. This is a valid argument. However, having identified the problem, it seems a pity that landscape designers then walk away from it. It would seem appropriate to monitor and evaluate the performance of native plantings and so develop principles for selecting species and subsequently maintaining them. CCAE is certainly one scheme worthy of more rigorous study.

THE FERN HILL TECHNOLOGY PARK

Almost inevitably, however, in an urban or suburban development, a planting design will include both native and exotic species. The Fern Hill Technology Park, which is developing east of the CCAE campus, demonstrates an attempt to blend native and exotic into a broadly naturalistic design. The site of 37ha (92.5 acres) is being developed to 'provide distinctive, comfortable accommodation for organizations in the technology industry in a prestigious landscaped setting.' (Fig. 7.13).

When fully developed, in 1994, the Park will be host to some 160 organizations employing about 3000 people. The site was selected because of its accessibility from both the ANU and the CCAE. Technology or science parks are a recent and burgeoning phenomenon in the developed world. As previously discussed, Stirling University has added one to its campus (pp. 108–9). Their broad aim is to bring together academic and applied research teams in order to develop marketable products. The development brief at Fern Hill, for example, calls for flexible spaces which could encompass administration, sales, demonstration, education and training, service, research and development, as well as laboratory work and assembly.

To meet these rather numerous requirements the site layout is based on clusters of three to five individual buildings grouped around a shared forecourt area. Fingers of planting separate these clusters and provide a physical and visual skeleton to the site. The landscape consultants prepared two documents. An overall site control plan located building groups, road layouts and overall site structure, and this was reinforced by a set of design guidelines. These addressed each critical design issue and set a framework in which the architects for the individual buildings could work.

The landscape guidelines aim to build on the existing landform and vegetation, whilst introducing elements to enhance the attractiveness, or image, of the park. Existing enclosure from the ridge-line on the east and north is reinforced by additional and new mass planting. Similarly the southern edge, along the main access link, Hayden Drive, is heavily planted. This planting opens out to reveal views of a water feature, which emphasizes the park entrance. From here, and within the site, the ridge-line planting provides a natural backdrop to the evolving development and apparently continues the existing surrounding woodland. It also provides shelter from the wind. The seemingly-natural planting then merges into the more formal character of the built development. The lake is also treated in a natural manner, to provide both visual interest and a useful amenity for employees.

These common areas of the park are the shared responsibility of the developer and the building tenants. When development is complete, Lend Lease, the developers, will withdraw from the management company, leaving all the tenants jointly responsible. An estate manager is employed to co-ordinate and organize the management and maintenance. Although this person's primary job is to look after the common areas, there are three additional roles – to negotiate the management of the individual sites; to participate in design and construction of new project work; and to maintain areas awaiting future development. If all these objectives can be achieved, the park should appear as a unified and planned development as it progresses through development phases to a completed working environment. It should also be easier to meet the overall goals of the landscape plan in creating a natural-looking development apparently set into an existing piece of woodland.

This chapter has used Canberra to demonstrate how landscape design can be creatively and usefully used in shaping and managing the living, working and leisure environment of a community of upwards of 250,000 people. Whilst the political energy needed to establish such a community has waxed and waned, the landscape designers

have generally adhered to the goals of the original plan prepared by Griffin in 1912. Obviously it has been adjusted to meet changing demands, and has been extended in area to meet growth in population. But by respecting his eye for topography, and following Weston's bold experiments with planting, the successors have brought the plan to life.

7.13 **Fern Hill Technology Park provides an efficient and pleasant setting for new hi-tech offices.**

8

Summary

The vision that all designers of fine landscapes must have in their mind's eye can be physically realized only by following a rigorous process. This process will be personal to each designer, but to achieve an acceptable solution it must establish and then satisfy certain basic criteria. The most important elements would seem to be the site, the brief, construction and planting techniques, and an involvement in the evolution of the scheme once the initial contract is completed and handed over to the users.

The site is felt by many to be the most important factor influencing design. Each site is different, and unless it is carefully studied and each individual idiosyncrasy recorded and evaluated, its personality or *genius loci* will escape the designer. Check lists for site surveys and evaluations are useful tools, but they must be adapted to suit the particular site and the particular use for which it is intended. Simmonds describes how early Japanese designers would live on a site for at least a year before beginning their design.[1] The pressure of today's largely market-orientated projects deny a designer such time – design exercises for commerce are constrained to weeks rather than months. A site visit may be extremely cursory and made during uncharacteristic weather conditions. However, tools such as stills, satellite, aerial and infra-red photography and videos can supplement, and partly compensate for, any shortfalls in site visits.

It is nevertheless of paramount importance that the designer understands the site in its context. Too often the ownership boundary becomes an opaque barrier at which the survey stops. But just as no man is an island within a society, so each site has a relationship, a continuity (or in the case of derelict land, a discontinuity) with the surrounding land. Water, soil and vegetation patterns will extend beyond the site, wildlife and humans will not perceive a barrier at the ownership line and the effects of climate will be common over a wider area.

Although it is useful in understanding a site to abstract certain elements, such as soils or vegetation, if it is to be intimately understood, it is necessary to draw a very detailed plan of the site – and the immediate surroundings – as it actually is. Through the process of plotting, measuring and recording, a spatial appreciation of the site develops, along with an insight into particular relationships between elements. Special places or conditions become apparent and the designer begins to see and feel the site and can decide how best it should be manipulated to accept the changes inherent in the brief.

An equally rigorous appraisal of the brief is also required from the designer. The client's demands must be challenged to ensure that they are realistic, achievable and necessary. Here an understanding of the social, economic and cultural context of the site is essential in order to assess the impact of the proposed change on both the local and wider community. Certain developments may benefit particular interest groups but damage others, and these facts should be evaluated and judged at an early stage in the design process. A change in the brief can often lead to less damaging requirements. Alternatively an early critical synthesis of the brief can demonstrate that the project should not occur in this particular location, as the site cannot accommodate it without suffering irreparable damage. But the most important result from this synthesis between site and brief is to identify the key issues that will most influence the design. These are the factors germane to the particular design project, and which will generate the basic structure and layout of the proposals. They may arise from design imagery, site conditions or client needs. Throughout the design process possible concepts and solutions must be tested against these issues to ensure that their requirements are being met.

Choice of construction methods and materials and of plants and planting techniques will depend on both the particular characteristics of the site and the functional requirements built into the brief. Does the designer wish to respond to the local vernacular in terms of materials or to the factory-made finishes of the buildings for which the design provides a setting? Choice of plant species and the size of stock used will similarly result from an assessment of site and users. Native species, planted as whips or seedlings may seem appropriate in a rural context. For a city centre plaza adjoining a company head office, specially prepared large nursery trees of exotic species may be more in keeping with the aspired corporate image.

The way in which plant and construction materials will change with time is also an important design consideration. This is influenced by level of expected use, capital cost for the project and the anticipated maintenance budget and management personnel. Where possible the landscape management team should be involved in the design process, to ensure that future management implications are recognized and accepted. The designer will most frequently attempt to produce a scheme that can be established and maintained using the current methods and procedures of the management team. If, however, the design calls for different horticultural or silvicultural skills, these must be clearly indicated and working methods and revenue costings discussed and agreed with the manager and the client.

At Warrington new town for example, the design objective was to establish a landscape structure of native woodland surrounding and penetrating the housing area. During establishment the landscape design and management were in the same section of the new town development corporation. This meant that the rather innovative design objectives were understood by the management team and their direct labour squad. Similarly any problems encountered in establishment or maintenance could be discussed with the designer and an agreed compromise reached between them.[2]

Regrettably this creative and sensible system did not survive when responsibility for open-space management passed to the local authority, despite several joint workshops and seminars. As a consequence the new town is now handing over all areas of woodland, other than amenity open spaces, to the Woodland Trust. This is a national voluntary organization that purchases and manages native woodlands threatened by neglect or development. This recognition and use of the Trust's skills in woodland management by Warrington is an interesting concept. It seems an appropriate body to ensure the long-term well-being of this new and innovative landscape structure.

As mentioned in chapter 1 the use of trusts to manage parks was used in Sydney, both in this century and the last. Increasingly, local government is unwilling and unable to cope with the long-term management of new parks and open spaces. Even with existing areas, as in Barrowfield in Glasgow, landscape management responsibilities are being passed over to residents. These are trends that the designer must be aware of, and he or she should realize that often the client will not ultimately be responsible for site maintenance. This calls for clear documentation of medium- and long-term management objectives to illustrate the design aims, and the maintenance principles and techniques by which they will be achieved.

It is also important that the landscape designer has a continuing involvement with the management team. For example at Bicentennial Park in Sydney the landscape architect is one of the trustees, and so can strongly influence park policies in the future. Many of the problems at Stirling University could have been avoided if the university had retained in an advisory role the consultants who produced the master plan. (The University has since appointed a landscape consultant to reappraise the campus design and management.) This monitoring role can often be a salutory experience for the designer when unforeseen problems arise several years after the contract is completed. Such problems are usually better and more economically solved by the original designer, who already understands the site, the client and the manager. An annual site inspection, undertaken with the landscape manager, followed by a written report to the client will in most cases be sufficient to ensure that the landscape design grows, changes and evolves sympathetically to the original design vision. Without such an annual check by the designer it is highly probable that the initial capital investment in the landscape project may be wasted through misapplied maintenance regimes.

This examination of completed projects has tested each against the landscape design process and discussed their strengths and shortcomings. It would appear that good designs broadly follow the steps of survey, analysis, synthesis, testing, construction and monitoring. If any part is weak or lacking, then the whole design falters. The process, however, is not a rigid, step-by-step formula to be dogmatically applied to each and every site. Rather it provides a framework, a set of guidelines, against which one can check, evaluate and test broad or detailed concepts as the design evolves. Probably the most important element is the often subjective design vision that must come from the individual landscape architect. This will fire the entire project. It must, however, be rigorously tested to ensure that it meets the key design issues synthesized from an analysis of site and brief. Then the designer, client and manager can be assured that the project will continue to satisfy and delight the users for years to come.

Notes

1 INTRODUCTION (*pp. 7–24*)

1 Lynch, Kevin; Sasaki Dawson and Demay, *Looking at the Vineyard. A visual study for a changing island*, Vineyard Open Land Foundation, 1973.

2 Laurie, Michael, *An Introduction to Landscape Architecture* (1st ed.), Pitman, 1975.

3 Colvin, Brenda, *Land and Landscape* (2nd ed.), John Murray, 1973, p. 110.

4 Moggridge, Hal, *Collaboration between Architects and Landscape Architects: Proceedings*, University of Edinburgh, 1986.

5 Weddle, Arnold, *Land Use and Landscape Planning*, Lovejoy, D. (ed.), Leonard Hill Books, 1973, p. 54.

6 Lynch, Kevin and Hack, G., *Site Planning* (3rd ed.), MIT Press, 1984.

7 Walker, Derek, *The Architecture and Planning of Milton Keynes*, Architectural Press, 1981, p. 133.

8 Rowe, Peter, *Design Thinking*, MIT Press, 1987, p. 96.

9 Steadman, Philip, *The Evolution of Designs*, LUP, 1979, p. 60.

10 Ibid. p. 2.

11 Alexander, Christopher, *A New Theory of Urban Design*, OUP, 1987, p. 58.

12 Steadman, op. cit., p. 207.

13 Schon, Donald, *The Design Studio*, RIBA Publications, 1985, p. 6.

14 Ibid. p. 76.

15 Ibid. p. 15.

16 Boardman, Philip, *The World of Patrick Geddes*, Routledge & Kegan Paul, 1978, pp. 261–6.

17 McHarg, Ian, *Design with nature*, Doubleday, 1969.

18 Hough, Michael, *City form and natural process*, Van Nostrand Reinhold, 1984.

19 Ibid. pp. 25–6.

20 Ibid. p. 19.

21 Handley, J.F., 'Landscape under stress' in *Ecology and Design in Landscape*, ed. Bradshaw *et al.*, Blackwell, 1986, p. 361–82.

22 Lynch, Kevin, *What time is this place?*, MIT Press, 1972, p. 212.

23 Jellicoe, Geoffrey, *The Guelph Lectures on Landscape Design*, University of Guelph, 1983, p. 158.

24 Whyte, William, *The Social life of small urban spaces*, Conservation Foundation, 1980.

25 Lynch, Kevin, *The Image of the City*, MIT Press, 1972.
Downs, Roger and Stea, David, *Maps in Minds*, Harper & Row, 1977.

26 Halprin, Lawrence, *RSVP Cycles: Creative Processes in the Human Environment*, George Braziller, 1969.
Burns, Jim, 'The *How* of Creativity: Scores and scoring' in *Lawrence Halprin: Changing Places*, ed. Neall, Lynne, San Francisco Museum of Modern Art, 1986, p. 40–59.

27 Jellicoe, op. cit., p. 65.

28 Ibid. p. 70.

29 Harrison, Lorna 'Bicentennial Park', *TAS* (Sydney), April 1986, p. 15.

30 Ibid.

31 Rowe, op. cit., p. 190.

32 Ward, Trevor, 'Threats to the Fauna and Flora of the Sydney Waterways' in *The Waterways of Sydney Symposium Proceedings*, Australian Marine Science Consortium.

33 Werwick, James, *Landscape Planning: Proceedings*, Canberra, 1982.

34 Boardman, op. cit., pp. 260–1.

35 Eckbo, Garrett, *The Landscape we see*, McGraw Hill, 1969.
Maragall, Pasqual, *Urbanisme a Barcelona: Plans cap al 92*, Ajuntament de Barcelona, 1988, pp. 118–24.

36 Samworth, Joe, 'Getting over Glasgow', *Landscape Design*, No. 176 (Dec. 1988), pp. 31–4.

37 Gibberd, Frederick, 'The Master Design: landscape, housing, the town centre' in *New Towns: The British Experience*, ed. Evans, Hazel, Charles Knight, 1972, p. 90.

38 Walker, op. cit., pp. 20–31.

39 Gustavsson, Roland and Tregay, R., *Oakwood's New Landscapes: designing for nature in the residential environment*, Warrington New Town Corporation, 1983.

40 Laurie, op cit.
Lynch, *Site Planning*.

41 Boardman, op. cit., pp. 317–19.
Australian National University, ANU, 1972.
Turner, John, *Campus, an American Planning tradition*, MIT Press, 1985.

42 Turner, ibid.

43 UNESCO, *Planning Buildings and Facilities for Higher Education*, Architectural Press, 1975, p. 46.

44 Boyer, Ernest, *College, the undergraduate experience in America*, Harper & Row, 1987, p. 32.

45 Chan, Judy, 'Development Plan for Stanford University' in *International Symposium on Campus Planning: Proceedings*, Ohio State University, 1986.

2. PARRAMATTA RIVER *(pp. 25–50)*

1   Lynch, Leonard, Spence, M. and Pearson, W., *Parameters for the River*, National Trust of Australia (NSW), 1975.
2   Sharpe, Gus, *The Rehabilitation of the Parramatta River*, National Trust of Australia (NSW), 1984.
3   Department of Environment & Planning, NSW, *Parramatta River: Regional Environmental Study : Open Space and Recreation*, Sydney, 1986.
4   Hope, R.M. (Chairman), *Report of the National Estate*, Australian Government Publishing Service, 1974.
5   Land Systems Pty Ltd, *Parramatta River 1983 : CEP/SGSP Project*, Department of Environment & Planning, 1983.
6   Forest, Warwick, 'Key factors for clean waterways' in *The Waterways of Sydney : Symposium Proceedings*, Australian Marine Science Consortium, 1988.
7   Land Systems Pty Ltd, *Wangal Centenary Bushland Reserve : Plan of Management*, Department of Environment & Planning, 1983.
8   Eskell, Rosalind, *et al.*, *A Bicentennial Park for Sydney*, Centre for Environmental Studies, Macquarie University 1978.

3. GEAR *(pp. 51–70)*

1   Middleton, Alan, in *Regenerating the Inner City : Glasgow's Experience*, ed. Dennison, D. Routledge & Kegan Paul, 1987, p. 29.
2   Kripp McLean Design Associates, *GEAR Environmental Maintenance Study : Part 2 – Operational Practices*, SDA, 1986.
3   Gillespie, William & Partners, *River Clyde Study*, SDA, 1979.
4   Cunning, James, Young, A. & Partners, *Barrowfield Case Study*, SDA, 1986.

4. DIPLOMATIC QUARTER *(pp. 71–93)*

1   Speer Plan, *Riyadh Diplomatic Quarter : Master Plan: Final Report*, High Executive Committee, KSA, 1978.

5. STIRLING UNIVERSITY *(pp. 94–116)*

1   Robert Matthew, Johnson-Marshall & Partners, *Stirling University Development Plan Report*, RUMJUM, 1968, p. 37.
2   SDA and Central Region, *Stirling University Innovation Park*, SDA Marketing brochure (undated).

6. TELLURIDE *(pp. 117–133)*

1   Fetter, Richard L. and Suzanne, *Telluride : from pick to power*, Caxton Printer, Idaho, 1982.
2   Abbey, Edward, 'Telluride Blues – a hatchet job' in *The Journey Home. Some words in defense of the American West*, E.P. Dutton, 1977, pp. 119–30.
3   McAllister Rinehart & Ring, *Telluride Feasibility Study*, Telluride Ski Corporation, 1971.
4   Ibid.

5   Ibid.
6   Abbey, op. cit.
7   Ski Magazine, 1983.

7. CANBERRA *(pp. 134–52)*

1   Latham, M.M.B. 'The City in the Park', *Landscape Australia* 3, 1982, p. 249.
2   NCDC, *Canberra : from limestone plains to Garden City*, 1986, p. 5.
3   Werwick, James, 'The Potency of the Griffin Plan', *Landscape Australia*, 1988.
4   Latham, op. cit. pp. 242–3.
5   Clough, Richard, 'Landscape of Canberra : a review', *Landscape Australia* 3, 1982, p. 197.
6   NCDC, *Urban Open Space Guidelines*, Technical Paper 21, Jan. 1981.
7   Johnson, Roger, *Design in the Balance*, University of Queensland Press, 1974, p. 23.
8   Werwick, James, *The Potency of the Griffin Plan*, Walter Burley Griffin Memorial Lecture, Canberra, 1988.
9   NCDC, *Parliamentary Zone : Development Plan*, Jan. 1986, p. 20.
10 Ibid., p. 22.
11 Latham op. cit., p. 247.
12 Land Lease Development, *Fern Hill Technology Park Limited : Briefing for the position of Estate Manager*, Nov. 1988.

8. SUMMARY *(pp. 153–55)*

1   Simmonds, John, *Landscape architecture : the shaping of man's natural environment*, London, 1961.
2   Scott, David, *et al.*, 'Warrington New Town: an ecological approach to landscape design and management', in *Ecology & Landscape Design : 24th Symposium of the British Ecological Society*, Manchester 1983, ed. Bradshaw, A.D. *et al.*, Blackwell Scientific Publications, 1986.

Index